" AMERICAN RENEWAL!"

AMERICA the home of the free because of the brave is now being destroyed from within. The magnificence of the glory which she was founded is no longer around because we've all chosen different paths and hate.

AMERICAN MEANS A – absolutely M – master E – everything that's R – right WITH AN I CAN attitude.

There has to be a conclusion for all the hate, divisiveness and corruption in AMERICA before the great reckoning is beckoned forth.

Don't fall for the lies, deception that you've lived with in that hate godless last administration, we have a man who loves his country – WHY NOT GIVE HIM SUPPORT?

America is not republican, democrat or independent any longer – it's AMERICAN PATRIOTISM vs SOCIALIST HATRED.

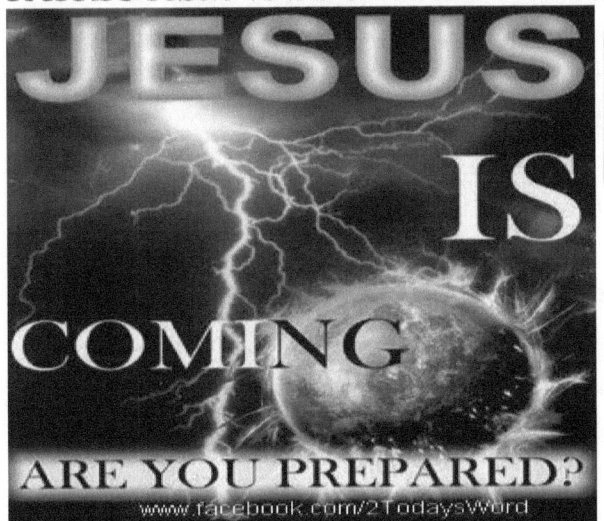

I0510263

Until we all become our best selves we will never truly understand

God's unconditional, unwavering love for us.

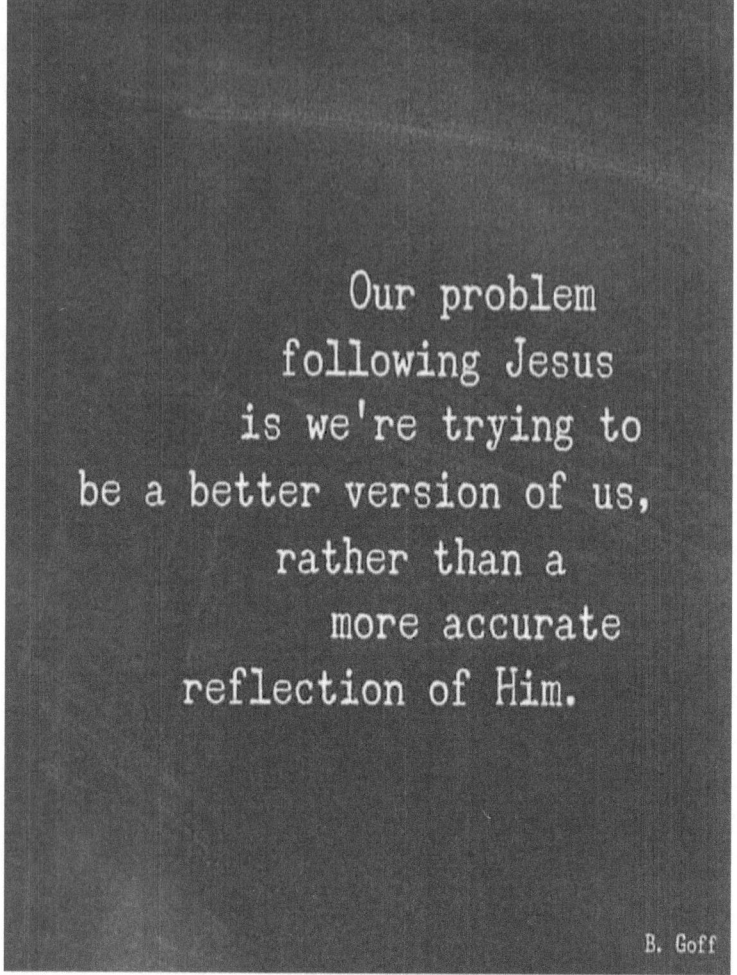

Our problem
following Jesus
is we're trying to
be a better version of us,
rather than a
more accurate
reflection of Him.

B. Goff

Learn to stand on your own feet, think for yourself and never be led by anyone but GOD. Look in the mirror often and see yourself. You are made in the image and likeness of God. LOVE YOURSELF ENOUGH TO TRUST YOURSELF.

There's no longer time to sit and watch, you better become as vocal as you can now if you value your freedoms, your life, your needs and your future. If you want them all you can not sit still and do nothing.

If you see a negative that equals a runaway

from it. If you are looking to figure things out for yourself – you must only look at the positive because only the positive is what's meant to be. The positive is all you need in life and you MUST make a choice now. Listen to only your heart and what is within you. Others will mislead you and reshape you. Be a thinker not a doer. Think your actions out before you get doing the wrong things. Your life only matters to you and God. How you shape it is up to you. If you want to help SAVE AMERICA start being optimistic. Stop being so me oriented and lend a hand to all those who need one. Your status, degrees, wealth or limitations can all be gone in a second. Your ability is what will drive you.

Find out if you can change enough to make a difference in your life and others and DO IT. Don't live just being satisfied. Live to be magnified in glory and the grandeur God set out for you. Can you achieve it? If you can achieve it – will you receive it and believe it? MAGNIFY GREATNESS. ELECTRIFY YOUR SOUL WITH POSITIVITY.

If you can muster up enough guts in your life to fight for what's right and help others when they are down then the American way of life will resume. God craves our love. Your father in Heaven is weeping for you because you won't say – YES honestly and mean it. Your heavenly father doesn't want FAKE and will not put up with disobedience. YOU MUST BE ACCEPTED BY JESUS CHRIST before you can go to your heavenly father. WHAT'S YOUR CHOICE GOING TO BE?

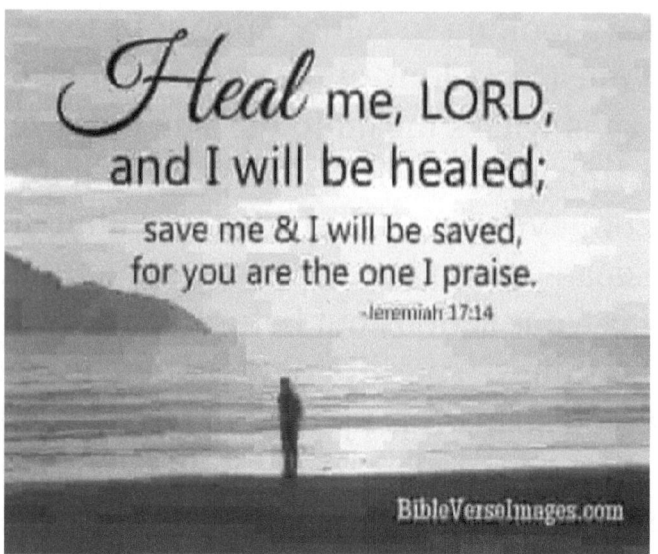

Heal me, LORD,
and I will be healed;
save me & I will be saved,
for you are the one I praise.
-Jeremiah 17:14

TAKE the leap of faith that you possess within yourself and strive to meet all your goals.

Be careful of what you entertain. SIN fascinates before it ASSASSINATES.

Why not trust yourself enough to make things work in your life? Why wait for someone to hand something to you that may not be good for you? May be you aren't meant for it. Evaluate your situation carefully and let go. Do your best with what you have and let God guide you forward.

If you only try in a positive way something will work. I am praying always and hoping for myself and things seem more positive. Never expect life to be anything more than possible. It stop expecting perfection.

I am writing this book not from a Democrat, Republican or Independent viewpoint. I am writing this from a personal viewpoint – a Conservative leaning Independent who is most definitely a TRUMP DEPLORABLE and staunchly CHRISTIAN human being. Yes, I am not that perfect human being or CHRISTIAN – GOD is still working on me.

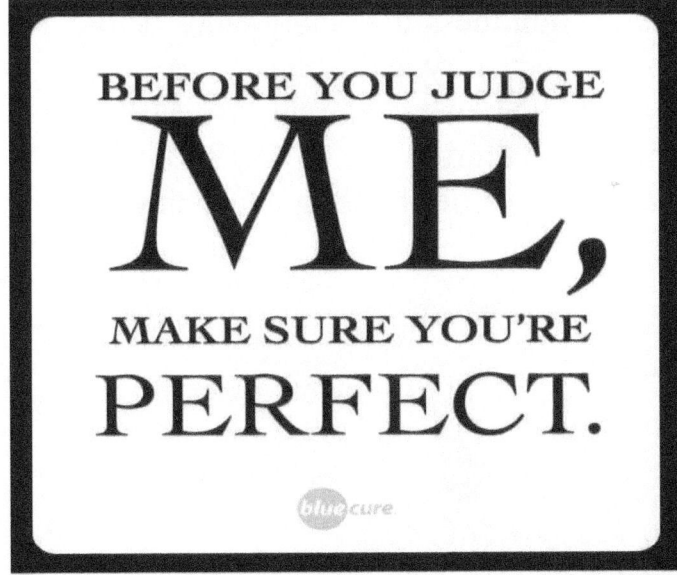

BEFORE YOU JUDGE
ME,
MAKE SURE YOU'RE
PERFECT.

blue cure

The view that I have had of my beloved AMERICA since childhood has disappeared because of only one major element – JESUS CHRIST.

As I have become much older now, lost my parents and my biological family is non – existent any longer, I can honestly state that the hope of a loving world is not an option any longer to me. I can not accept the divisiveness and hate. I have successfully beat cancer several times and see the light beyond the tunnel.

This is one of the main reasons that I am led to spread my hope and prayers for this NATION. It is not a religion America needs, it's Christian-Judaeo values that must return full force into each one of our lives. SAVE AMERICA is extremely important and I do believe that TRUMP is being led by God. Why would I feel that way someone asked?

It is because of several reasons alone. You see the POSITIVE backing of faith leaders of all faiths, you see the success achieved in cultures, you see the economic soundness in society, you see the optimism in personal reality and you see the CHRISTIAN attempts being made by TRUMP. Putting the embassy in Jerusalem, CHRIST back in Christmas and family values back in every day life.

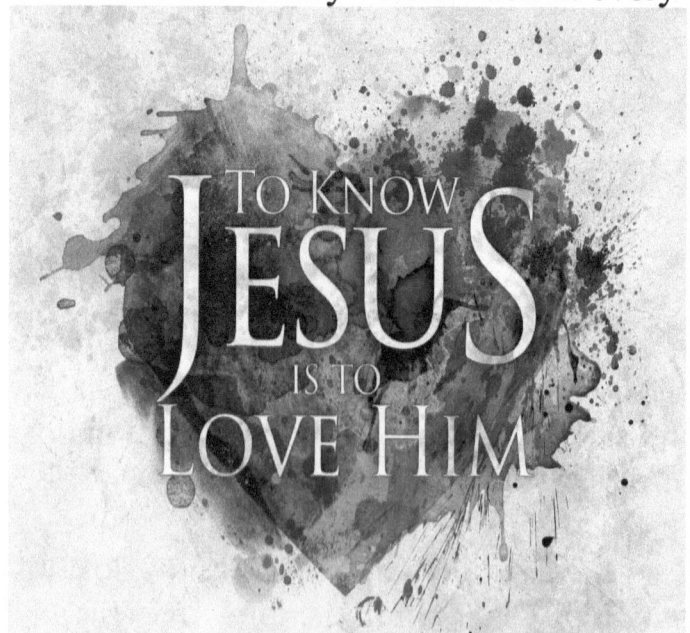

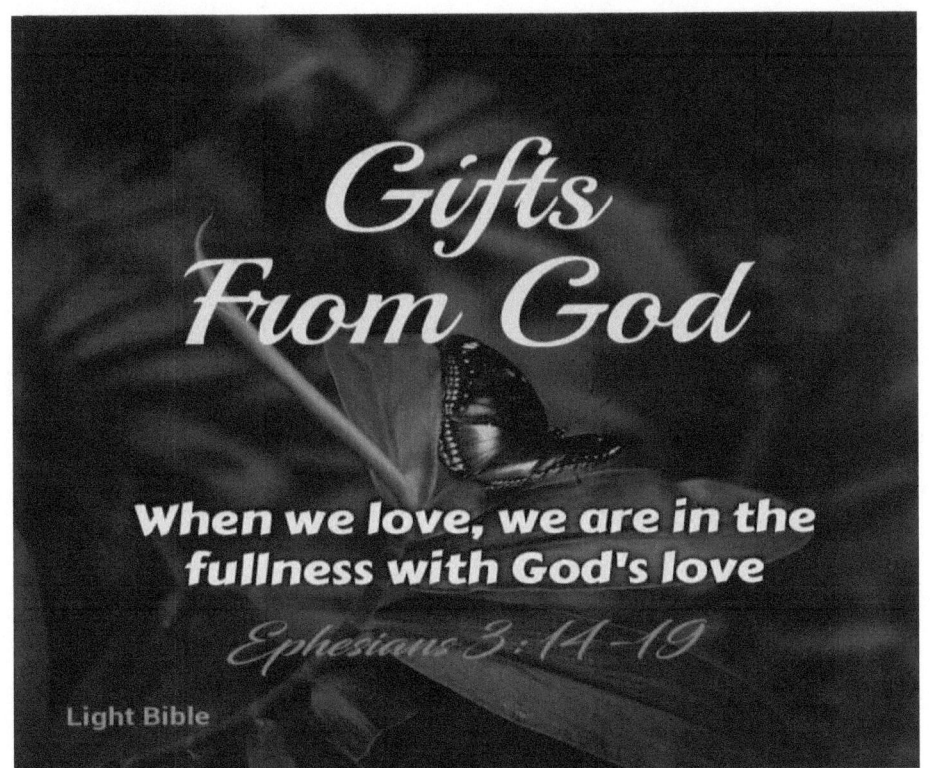

When we love, we are in the
fullness with God's love

Ephesians 3:14-19

Light Bible

It is not just one human beings responsibility to achieve the goals God has put us on earth to achieve. It is only God's judgment that we are responsible to at the end of our journey. If we do not attempt to make things right – that equals failure. So knowing this, WHY WOULD YOU CHOOSE TO FAIL?

Without great leadership, a great mindset and goals for success you will never receive what is meant for you in life.

Your journey is not an option it is your destiny to your eternity. Focus on making good choices for your destiny to be great and cast away all that is not positive now.

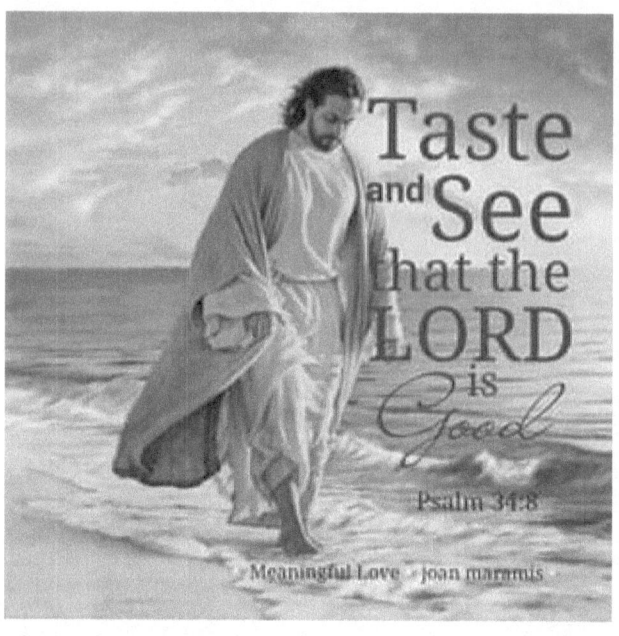

Taste and See that the LORD is Good

Psalm 34:8

Meaningful Love - joan maramis

If you are right in God's eyes you will know it.

LET others witness your efforts and emulate your joy. Why not feel like you've helped?

What do you see for America? With all the visceral hate, division and corruption how can life exist as God intended it to here in America. Is America beyond the ability to save?

Why can't the haters realize that those who they victimized for eight years in the last administration have had ENOUGH and want America to work as it was intended for all. It's power hungry people in D.C who will never be satisfied no matter what.

ALL Americans must become more humble and less expecting. Pray more for real and let the normal sequence of life happen and stop trying to control and manipulate everything according to YOU.

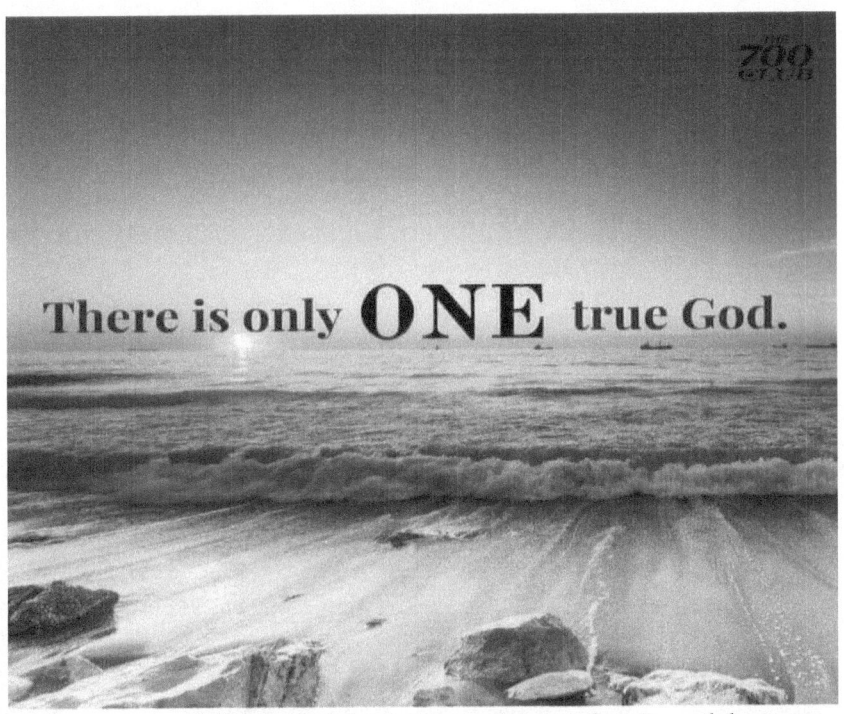

There is only ONE true God.

The Lord knows a fake, the Lord knows what's needed and if you seek sincerely you will find it all in this glorious country and in your soul.

Becoming inclusive is not the answer because the internal hate that consumes loss in not acknowledged by those continuing to spew it. Let go and let society and those who voted for a difference have their rights. Why are the haters the only one's permitted to have rights?

God is like OXYGEN.
You can't see Him,
but you can't live
WITHOUT Him!

©Godfruits.com

This is a total collision with reality is my personal view of what I see in America today. It is power grabbing bureaucrats that are never willing to relinquish authority and lust for fame versus future glory and personal achievement.

AMERICA is a profoundly great country. Those who feel otherwise should study their history, move and enjoy less opportunities and total control.

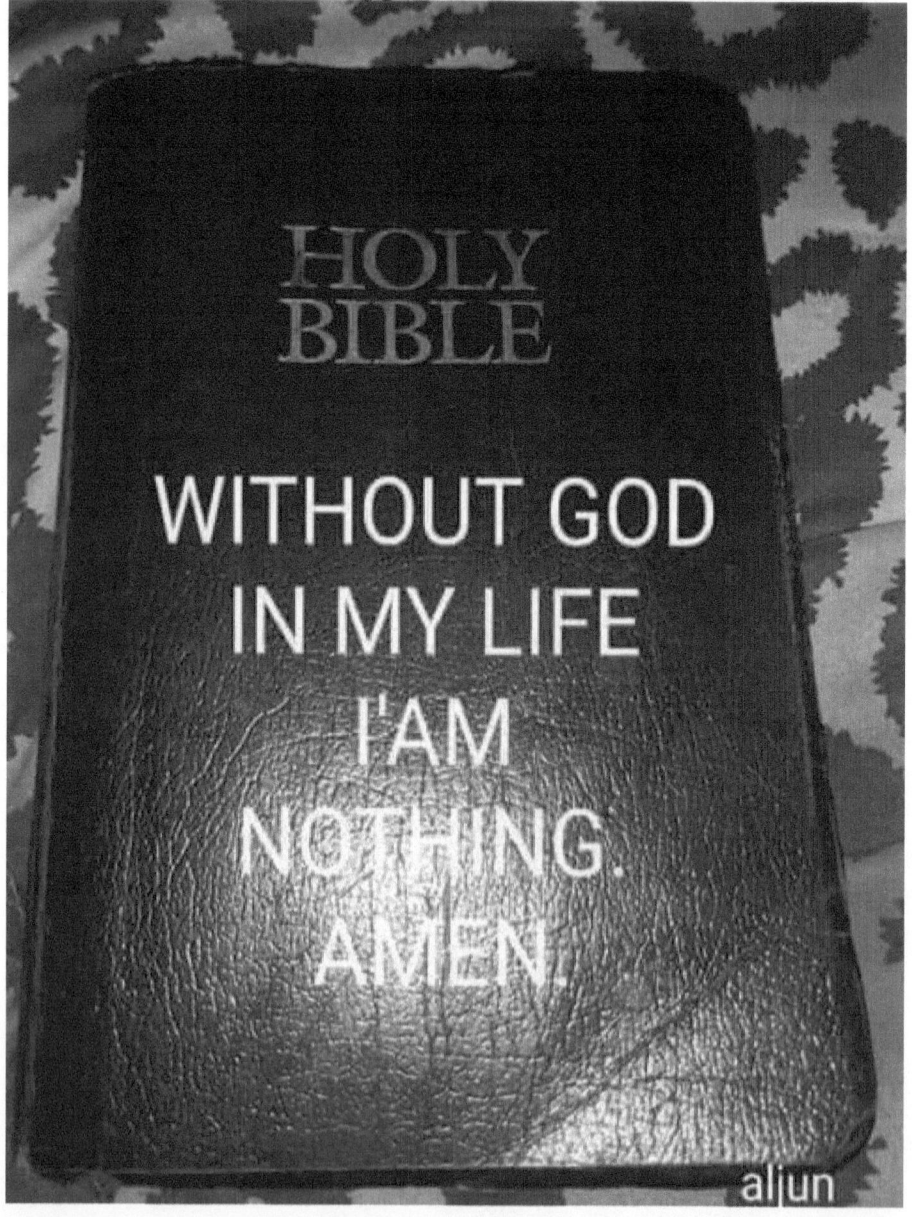

If the haters in society could just visualize what average Americans see in them, I believe that consciously they would hide. These hate filled devil oriented people will never be happy until they totally experience a reincarnation within themselves. They need to realize that hate will not survive. It's already been tested and proven a LOSER.

American society has changed so drastically that some say that it is going to almost be impossible to SAVE AMERICA.

The hate must go immediately if there is ever going to be a chance for AMERICA to be great again. America is truly a blessed nation. The diversity, the cultural and eclectic scope of America is awesome. Americans she feel blessed not hated to be able to live in a country like America.

BUT, unless we accept the founding father's principles and adhere to the greatness within ourselves and beg GOD to become number one in all aspects of life, there's little or no hope to SAVE AMERICA.

WE ARE ALL GOD'S CHILDREN and until each one of us accepts that premise – life will just be an existence. NO, God knows everything about us more so then we do. HE sees the hate, feels the anger and hypocrisy in the fake platitudes that the haters constantly spew. YES, he loves them too, but will also judge them as well. Walk the journey you want but; REMEMBER there's a day coming for accountability and destiny.

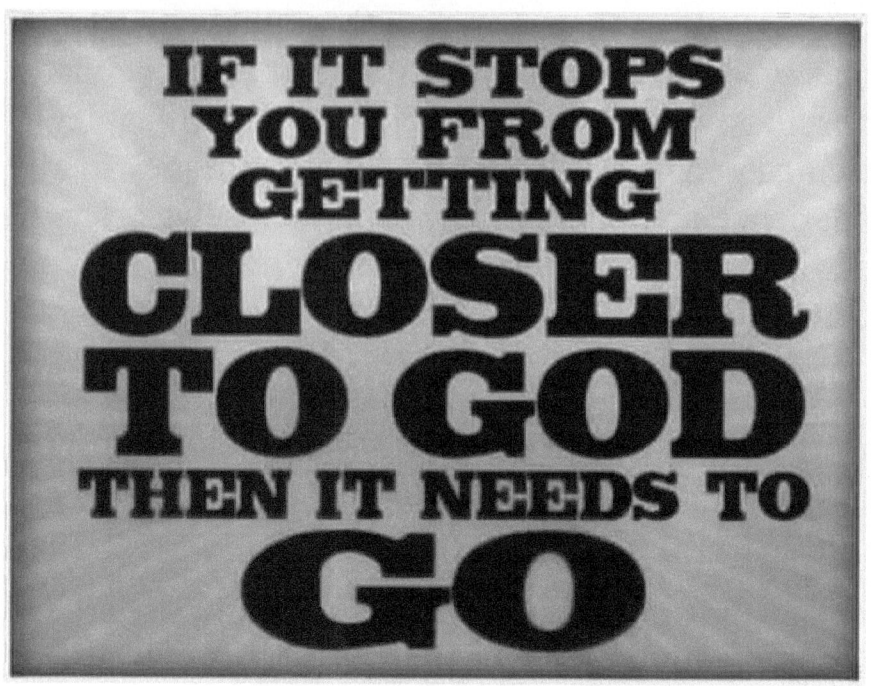

IF IT STOPS YOU FROM GETTING CLOSER TO GOD THEN IT NEEDS TO GO

Nothing FAKE is mistaken by God – because he knows everything about us and is in control. You are either for me or against me, says the Lord. If you espouse hate, infanticide, abortion at will, genocide, murder, violence or anything negative you are not a Christian following God's will.

You can't dance with the devil and be with the Lord too. Stop trying to stroke your ego and think society is stupid. God is going to be the ultimate victor in life.

When you see the HATE thrown around by the democrat party – you can be sure it isn't what God wants.

It is time for EVERYONE in America to read up on the history of America as it truly is and stop being "GROUP THINKERS." Nothing good can come of being a group thinker. Why do you want to think like others and not like yourself? Are you that insecure?

Yes, we have people in lead positions in government who have been there forever and hold very divisive stands in life. Do you admire people like that or are you that easy a person to dominate? Do you enjoy being a follower?

I would rather choose to follow a Godly kind eternal position of judgment at the end of my life and find out I was right all along, then to follow a life of lazy, hate filled me oriented ignorance and no thought of life after death and be wrong.

It's time to figure out where you are going and what your destiny will be in the end no before it's too late. Life doesn't last forever and there will be choices in life that will have consequences for your decisions. THINK FOR YOURSELF – NO ONE WILL BE WITH YOU IN THE END.

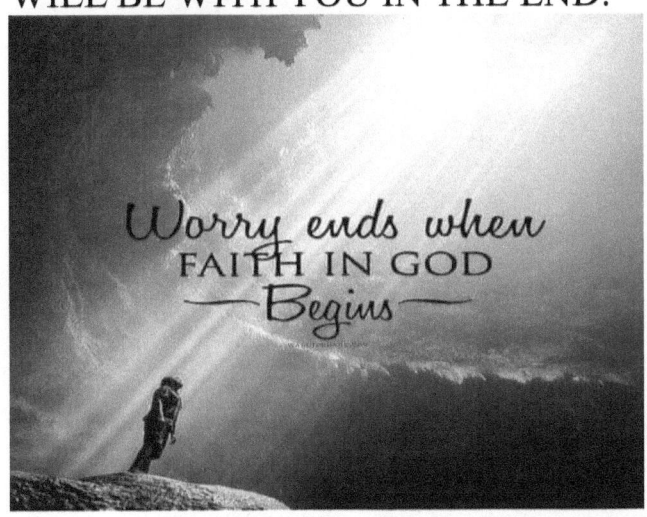

Hang your hat on the rack and realize your actions do matter. You will have to respond one day no matter if you do feel like an IMPERIAL MONARCH now.

If you choose to be a follower and do nothing but follow the leader, I hope you arrive at the right destination in the end. You don't get many chances in life to redo your steps, but if you do take that chance and aim for the positive.

Don't allow yourself to be influenced by others, influence yourself with a solid approach that is well thought out, a positive one hundred per cent for you and achieve the goals now.

Once you can attain for yourself a semblance of civility, understanding, trust, love and goodness within yourself, you will succeed.

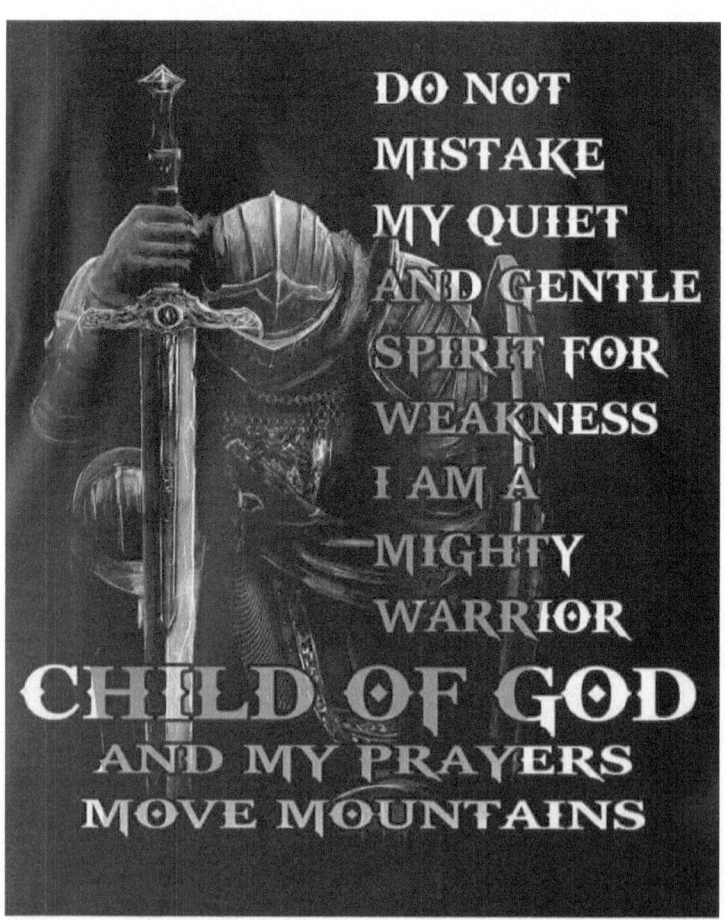

DO NOT MISTAKE MY QUIET AND GENTLE SPIRIT FOR WEAKNESS I AM A MIGHTY WARRIOR CHILD OF GOD AND MY PRAYERS MOVE MOUNTAINS

Come to the journey of life with a common sense

approach not an oh pity me attitude. Success is different for everyone and the journey you walk on is solely your responsibility.

I'm not sure where the democrat side of anything starts but; REALISM, HONESTY AND FACTS are the only source to attack it's negativity. I have never seen nor ever imagined a more HAND OUT CRAZE society as we are living in now. There's no excuses for it except GROUP THINKING, BRAIN TWISTING ILLOGICAL MANIPULATION and sheer cowardice.

If you do not become a well – rounded human being with confidence within yourself you can not expect success. 360 DEGRESS of well-roundness and conviction within yourself.

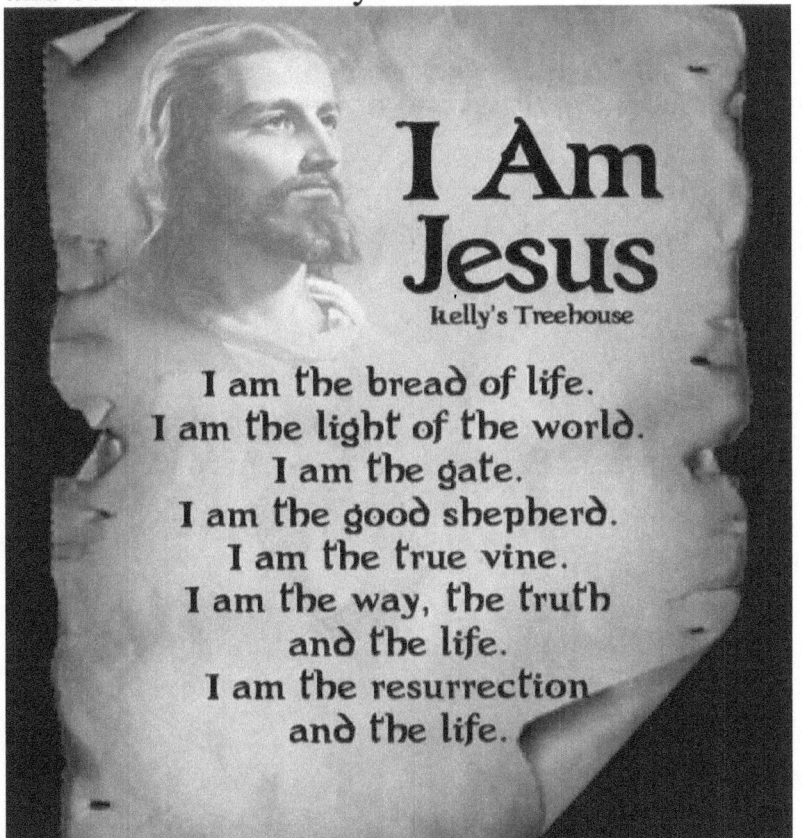

Find the guts within yourself to not only

love yourself but to trust yourself. Give yourself a chance in life. Never worry about failing. Never worry about issues. WALK with confidence and never give up. Don't let anyone determine the path you take.

AMERICANS chose a compadre who is a real business savvy intelligent human being striving for utter success for everyone – especially the silent majority.

AMERICANS wanted to change the course of history and discover the total potential in this country instead of being driven by individual choice by a few crooks.

It is the most profoundly stimulating success America has ever experienced in my lifetime. I have prayed that greatness could be accomplished through dedication, drive and brilliance – and now all I see is the hate filled losers trying to manipulate, destroy and take advantage of everything good that AMERICA exemplifies.

Why would you choose failure if success was a very viable option? Choose success. Live it and pass it on. We all have a heartbeat and aspirations in life. Find your passion and lead yourself in that direction. Sure you may stumble and fall many times, but get up and start over again.

Don't dream to mighty a dream – dream achievable dreams and master them always. God wants that for you. Let your own personal goals be achieved but don't trample on others while you are working to succeed. Work toward developing the content of your character with intelligence, great choices and charisma. You can reach your potential, but you need to make sure it's real not a baseless macho better then anyone attitude. Love yourself and others enough to want success for everyone. Share it, spread it and let go.

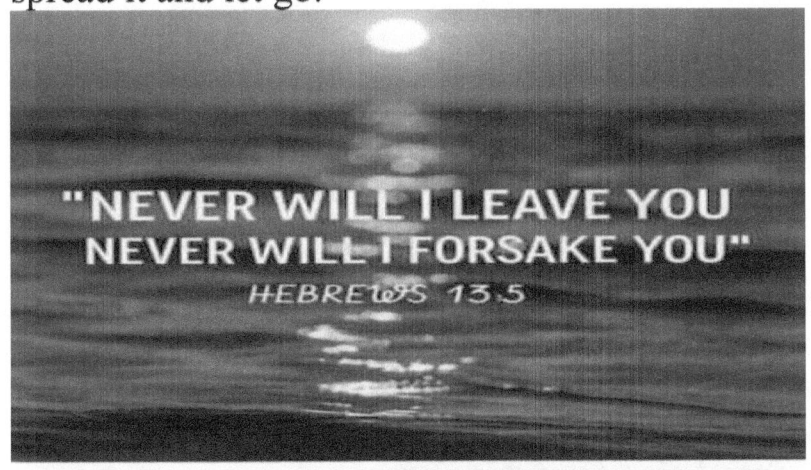

"NEVER WILL I LEAVE YOU NEVER WILL I FORSAKE YOU"
HEBREWS 13:5

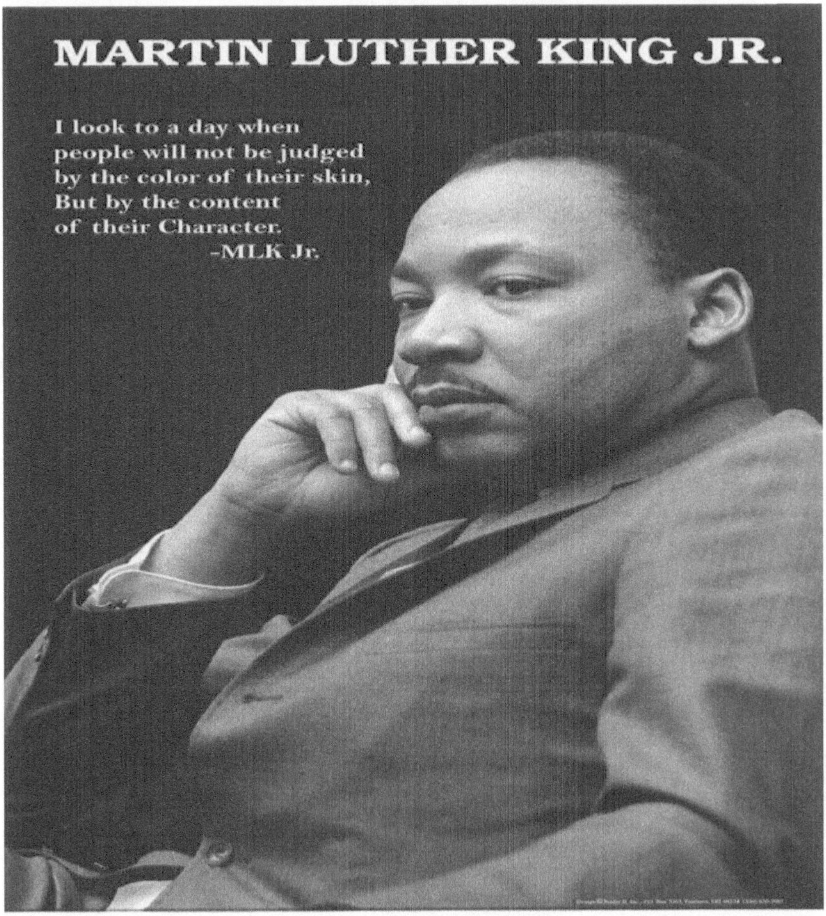

MARTIN LUTHER KING JR.

I look to a day when people will not be judged by the color of their skin, But by the content of their Character.
-MLK Jr.

America has had many wars, trials and an extreme amount of hate for generations. Living through many of them and knowing the meaning of all of the history – I can tell you that the education I have had makes me eternally grateful.

Knowing the dissension through all the carnage of my past and the values its taught me in life; I can say that the democrat party holds a terminal amount of responsibility for it.

Why relive the hate, division and decisiveness? Is it because of the hate, greed and globalist anxiety that the haters are promoting group thinking and stupidity? No one was meant to think for you. Stop being so gullible and create your life. No one owes you anything in life.

Find a source of greatness and focus on it. Feel your passions and reach for them. Pursue your greatness and pass it on.

We are one body in Christ Jesus, we do not stand alone but we have one goal if we are living for optimism truth and God.

All humans seek greatness and with help that is given naturally and genuinely the world can be saved. Feel the real presence within yourself.

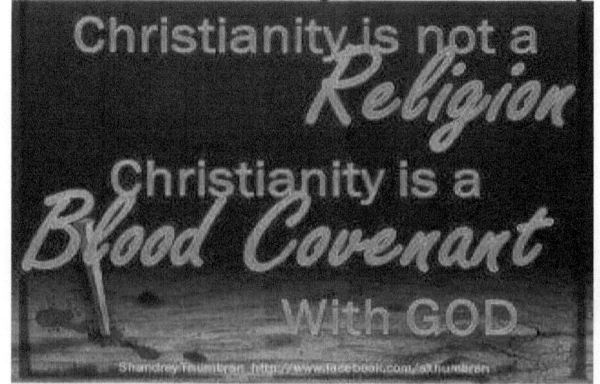

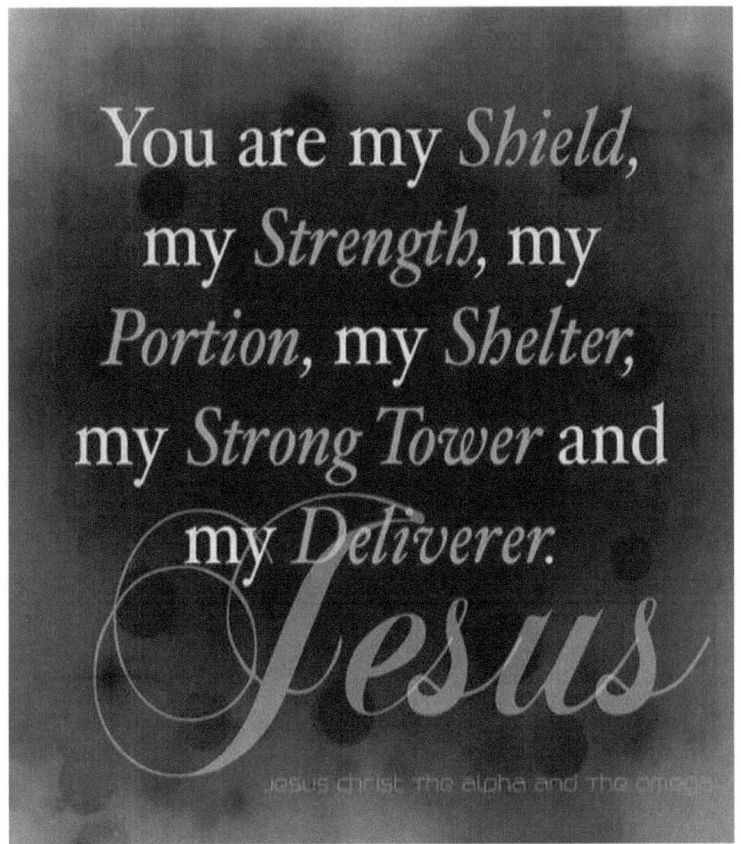

You are my *Shield*, my *Strength*, my *Portion*, my *Shelter*, my *Strong Tower* and my *Deliverer*. *Jesus*

jesus christ the alpha and the omega

Life will be what you set your course to so focus and feel.

Once you get your life in sink with the rhythm of your heartbeat and the goals you want to achieve you will see success. Add God to your life and you will soar. Stay positive and accept your issues and never expect yourself to master everything you attempt on the first shot. Mistakes strengthen and can teach you things not normally learned in life. Learn from all your mistakes, move on and let go. Forgive yourself and master what you need to.

Back when logic was understandable, decorum was expected and vulgarity severely not put up with in life, there was more of a life then. You knew what was expected of you and you never crossed the line because you knew you would pay in the end.

I don't know if it's just me, but; I do get very appalled at the nasty sex talk on social media. Maybe because I'm old or not with it is the reason. I feel if you can air your trash on social media what else will you do?

Do you really think people truly care about you that much? Do you base your choices on approval, acceptance and popularity? REMEMBER, you are one human being in the big scheme of things and you must focus on yourself and no one else.

It's not a hand out world. If you are expecting a hand out, I hope it is the right one for you and it can help you in life. Stop wasting your life wanting go do what you must to be receiving it all. Sometimes it hurts or there is pain on the way to your goal but; you must focus on your goal because your goal is not someone else's goal.

Make those who doubt you cringe when they see you succeed and invite them on your journey. Most likely, they will be horrified and speechless.

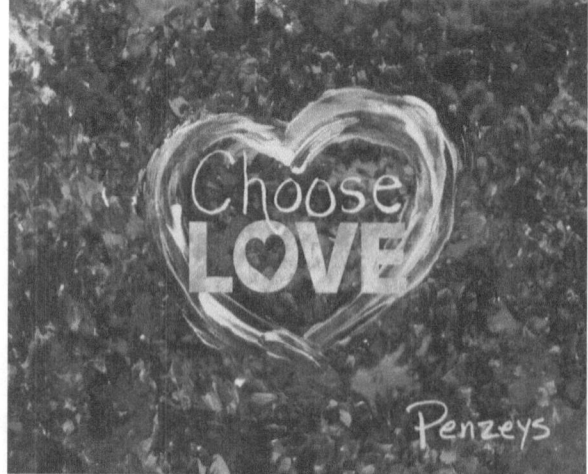

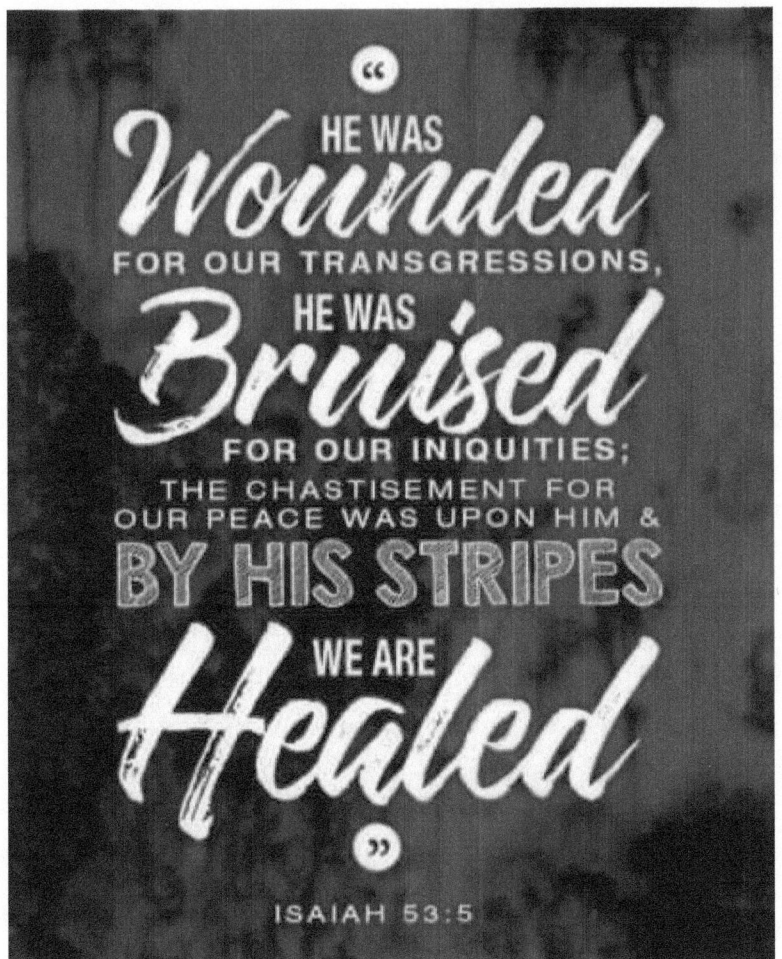

“
HE WAS *Wounded*
FOR OUR TRANSGRESSIONS,
HE WAS *Bruised*
FOR OUR INIQUITIES;
THE CHASTISEMENT FOR
OUR PEACE WAS UPON HIM &
BY HIS STRIPES
WE ARE *Healed*
”
ISAIAH 53:5

Jesus knows everything about you and knows what's best for you, but you must call on him and beg him to be the master of your life. There's no fake with JESUS.

No matter how long and how far you've strayed from Jesus he will always forgive you. Do not make excuses for not being right with Jesus – it's your choice that led you away.

You can always find your way to your own peace if you let go and let yourself do what's right. Let yourself be happy and don't worry what others feel, life will go on no matter what.

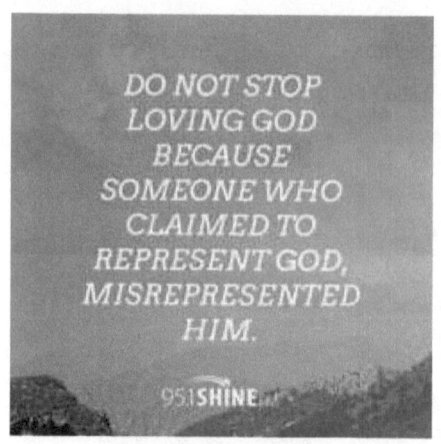

DO NOT STOP LOVING GOD BECAUSE SOMEONE WHO CLAIMED TO REPRESENT GOD, MISREPRESENTED HIM.

95.1SHINE

You were born with free will and choice and Jesus wants you to make the choice to come to him.

I was raised with a father who expected dignity and behavior that was dignified at all times. Sure I had a lot of fun, laughs and fabulous adventures, but; I was never around trashy low life's like those in the democratic – hate mongering crowd.

I was taught if you can't do it in front of GOD you better not do it.

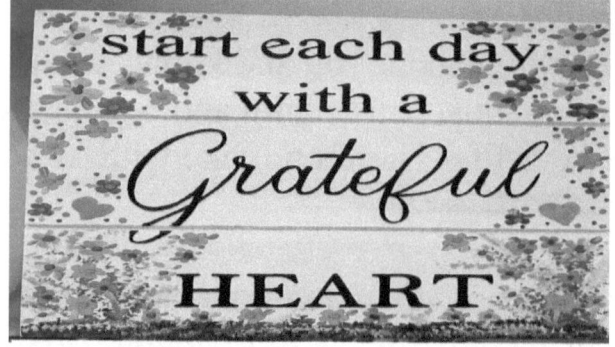

start each day with a *Grateful* HEART

There's so much talk about "SAVING AMERICA" nowadays, but; before you can save America you have to save yourselves.

When the government decided to control every facet of your existence is when American society was on the decline. When God was removed from schools – schools became a mess. When sanctity was ignored everything went down hill. Especially when abortion at will was acceptable behavior, free choice to kill a child after birth was a right – that's when Jesus Christ cried.

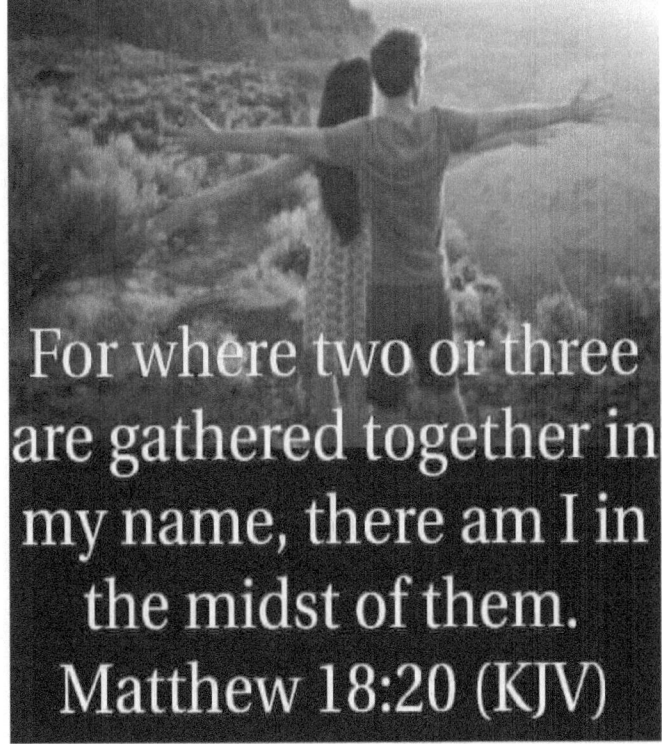

For where two or three are gathered together in my name, there am I in the midst of them.
Matthew 18:20 (KJV)

Prayer is the only way to SAVE AMERICA and be right in God's eyes.

It's a sad fact – or just a plane collision with reality that the forever politicians can't handle losing control. As an AMERICAN of immigrants and patriots of America, it becomes almost an embarrassment to normal thinking humans how LOW these people will go. HEARING THE CRIES of people afraid of losing America and seeing the destruction they will go to – to get their egocentric nauseating minds placated is truly a collision with insanity.

How can you SAVE AMERICA when you have hate driven power obsessed do nothing but waste money and seem to never lose the lust for power losers in the government who pretend to be God-fearing and vote for Godless infanticide, genocide, abortion at any time, criminal lovers? ONLY GOD CAN. Power hungry – destruction is what humans see now in government and IF WE DON'T STOP AND REMEMBER GOD WILL BE VICTORIOUS not them – there's no solution.

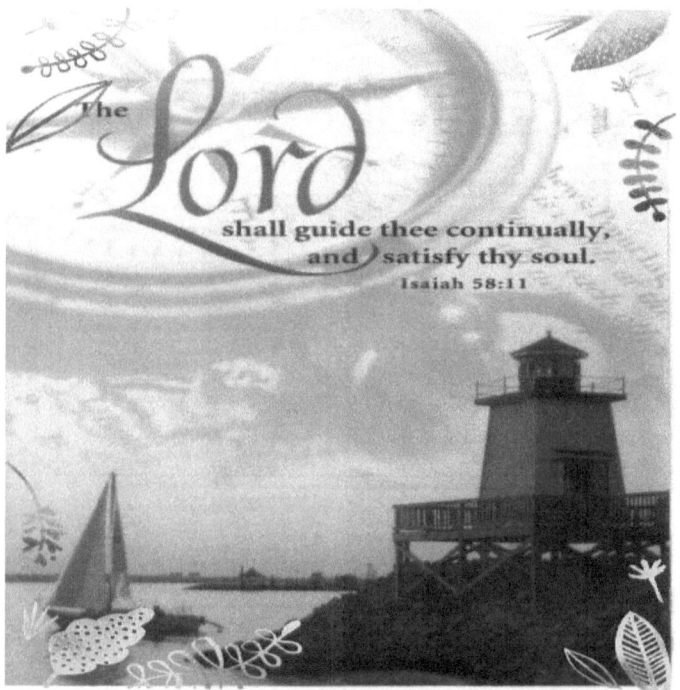

PRAY WITHOUT CEASING and let the American people's voices be heard.

AMERICA was founded on Christian – Judaeo values and we have traveled so far away from that, that only prayers and effort to regain our moral values can SAVE AMERICA..

The bigots, the haters and the immoral zealots must be vanquished fast if you want to SAVE

AMERICA. It's not a joke what the politically elite ignorant people in America are doing in avoiding reality. When are you going to face your reality?

Waking up to the fact that no one really cares accept you about your existence should make you aware of your finiteness in life.

It is you who hold the key to your destiny not your parents, the government or anyone. The fact that your alive is a blessing and that blessing must be honed in and beautified by you and passed on.

It makes no difference what went on in the past – it is today and that is the only thing you can control right now. Make your today the best you can and do not expect any kudos from anyone. You aren't entitled to any and most likely if you get any it will be very circumspect at best.

Let yourself soar with trust in your soul and belief in yourself without limitation. Succeed for yourself. I have had to in life and so can you. Having

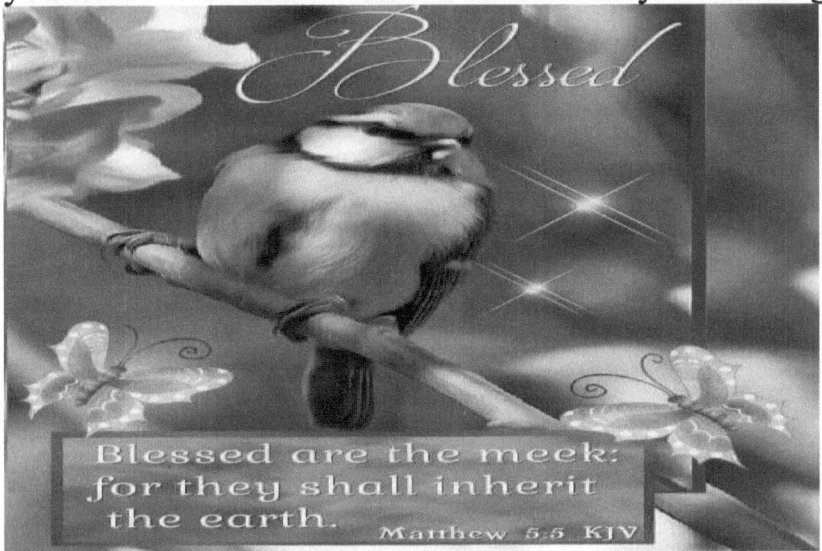

Blessed are the meek: for they shall inherit the earth. Matthew 5:5 KJV

no human genetic being in your life can be an

advantage to you. It was in my case. All the negative is finally gone from my past and placed in God's hands.

The elite in D.C are so far off base that God no longer wants to know who they are because they prowl around their cubby holes with satanic venues, vengeful actions and self-oriented platitudes of glory and fail to acknowledge their personal worth.

Make sure you choose the best option in life to become the best you. Be careful if you choose to follow someone else. If you choose to be a follower and not a leader – I hope you get to the right destination point in your life.

In my lifetime, I've not really ever found any great follower to be very successful or interesting enough for me to want to follow them.

No matter how many mistakes you make in life, there are always others in life who have made more then you. GET UP, START OVER and learn by all your mistakes – nothing is terminal but – death.

How can anyone SAVE AMERICA even with the best of intentions with the vile ignorance of hate and lust predominating every action.

Education means NOTHING if you can't balance it with common sense. Status is nothing if you can't use it for any sound action. Blithering idiots don't make a sound that is tolerable to any species on earth.

Never focus on what you hold focus on

what you achieve. If you go on in life thinking that you are no good because you haven't got something someone else has – you will never succeed.

Most of the time, if you pursue things that are a passion of yours – and truly achieve them that will be what is most important for you. REMEMBER ALWAYS PASS ON TO OTHERS, WHATEVER YOU CAN TO HELP THEM.

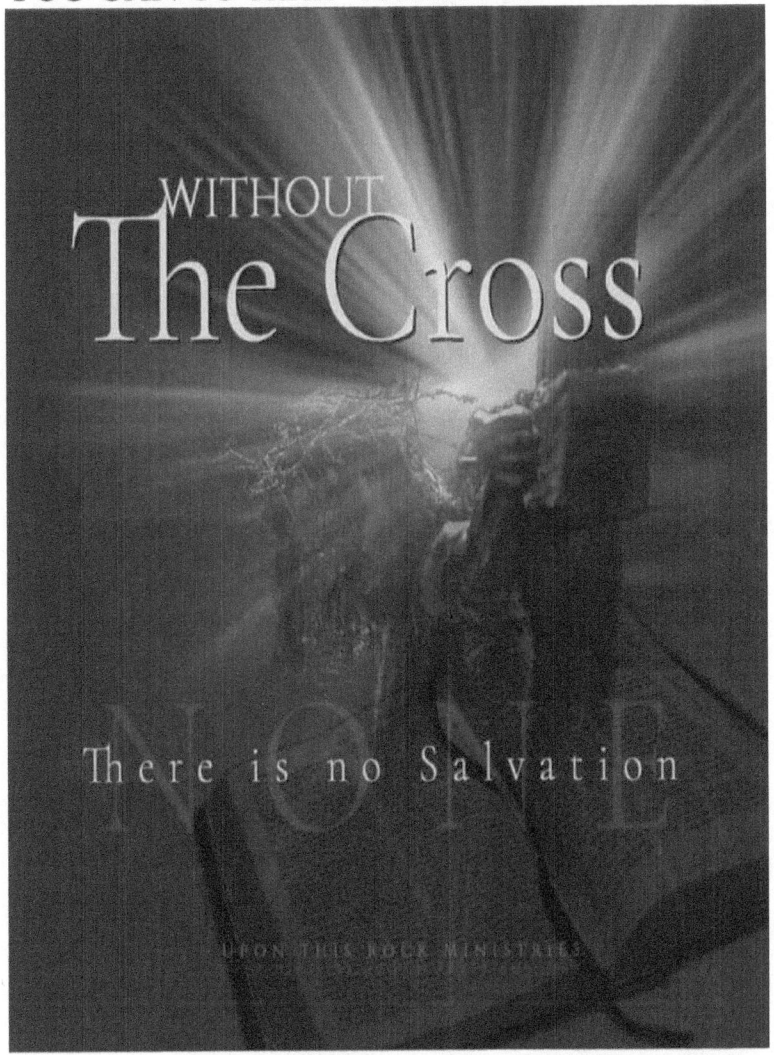

WITHOUT The Cross

There is no Salvation

NONE

UPON THIS ROCK MINISTRIES

REMEMBER, try to find a morally sound place for you to occupy in your mind and maintain it. It's a place where all things are working in sink and create a peace within you.

Moral valor should not always be attributed to a faith – religious base but rather a faith concept within yourself and your ability to thrive.

Why not stun the world and make your statement obvious just by example and actions you take in life. Let the world see yourself succeed and make a statement of value that will be appreciated and affect others positively.

Look for the best in life and nurture it fully. Focus on the elements that will work in your life and master them fully.

SO WE DO NOT FOCUS ON WHAT IS SEEN BUT WHAT IS UNSEEN. FOR WHAT IS SEEN IS TEMPORARY, BUT WHAT IS UNSEEN IS ETERNAL.
2 CORINTHIANS 4:18

The only way to SAVE AMERICA is to put an END to handouts, wants and unearned issues in life. STOP ACCEPTING ignorance as bliss and cop outs and normal behavior. Grow up and become pro-active with your life.

Remember the days when those who wished to live in America were filled with hard work, perseverance. Remember what they survived through to do so. IT'S HISTORY and maybe HISTORY should become a REQUIREMENT to graduate from any school in America. AMERICAN HISTORY must be revered not ignored or destroyed. Yes, things happened, but look where you are at today.

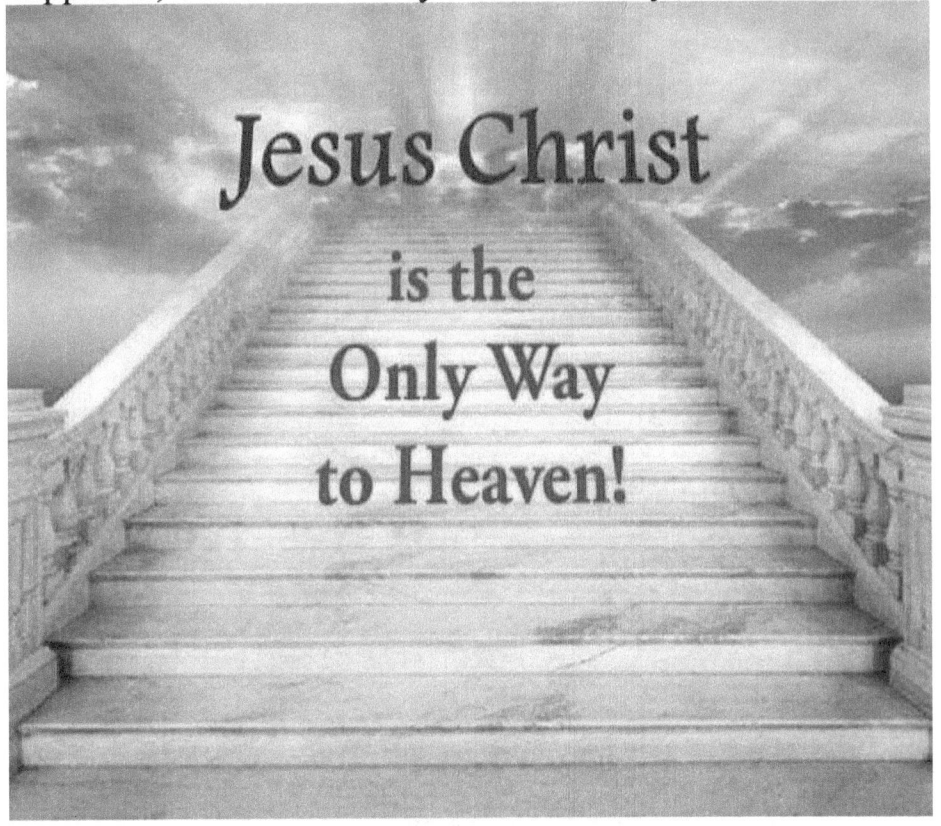

Stop being an enabler, a passifier or revisionist. History is history and strength has come out of most of America's History. Remember those who carved the statues of all the historical figures and their love and commitment to America. Be grateful not hateful.

No one is owed a thing in life just because you breathe.

Wars, slaves, hate, violence and many things have occurred in America but; before society became so selfish, self-oriented and self-placating there was understanding and moral values. It's so far from what Martin Luther King Sr ever imagined. It's so far away from the days of acceptance and Godliness. Put God back into life and stop expecting anything. Help don't hinder. Work together as one – not a group of one. Yes, I call those haters, bigoted, me oriented government officials a group of one. One voice of hate, one thought of power versus greatness and one voice to horrify God.

If you want to SAVE AMERICA – first stop making Christ Jesus cry. If you can't do it in front of him – don't do it at all..

The time is now and the question for you is when. Get up and make a difference in your life now before its too late. Stop expecting and start getting what you seek. GO AFTER IT WITH VENGEANCE. Accept a failure if you do not succeed the first time and redo your steps. ONLY YOU WILL ACHIEVE the goals you desire in life. Each one of us is on our own journey. BE AN EXAMPLE.

We can walk this journey successfully as respected individuals or as sad no action people. Life is filled with choices and each choice holds its own consequence. Don't be a victim to inaction and the negative, be victorious and overcome what you must in your life to satisfy your inner being.

Learn to deep breathe, let go, think and proceed with confidence. Faith in yourself with conviction.

A Prayer to *Forgive* when you can't *Forget*

Father, I lay down (person's name) to You. Lord, I'm having a hard time forgiveing them. God, I want to forgive, but the pain keeps me from moving forward. But today, I choose to give it to You...the pain, the bitterness, the desire for revenge. I give it all to You. Lord, heal every part of me that is being affected by this situation. I release them to You now. In Jesus' name, Amen

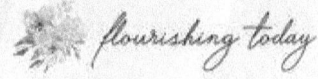 flourishing today

Let go of what you must and move on before it's too late.

"AWAKEN YOURSELVES!"

      The day JESUS cried was the day you denied him. Why not accept the Lord and totally surrender what is inside you? START ENJOYING YOU.

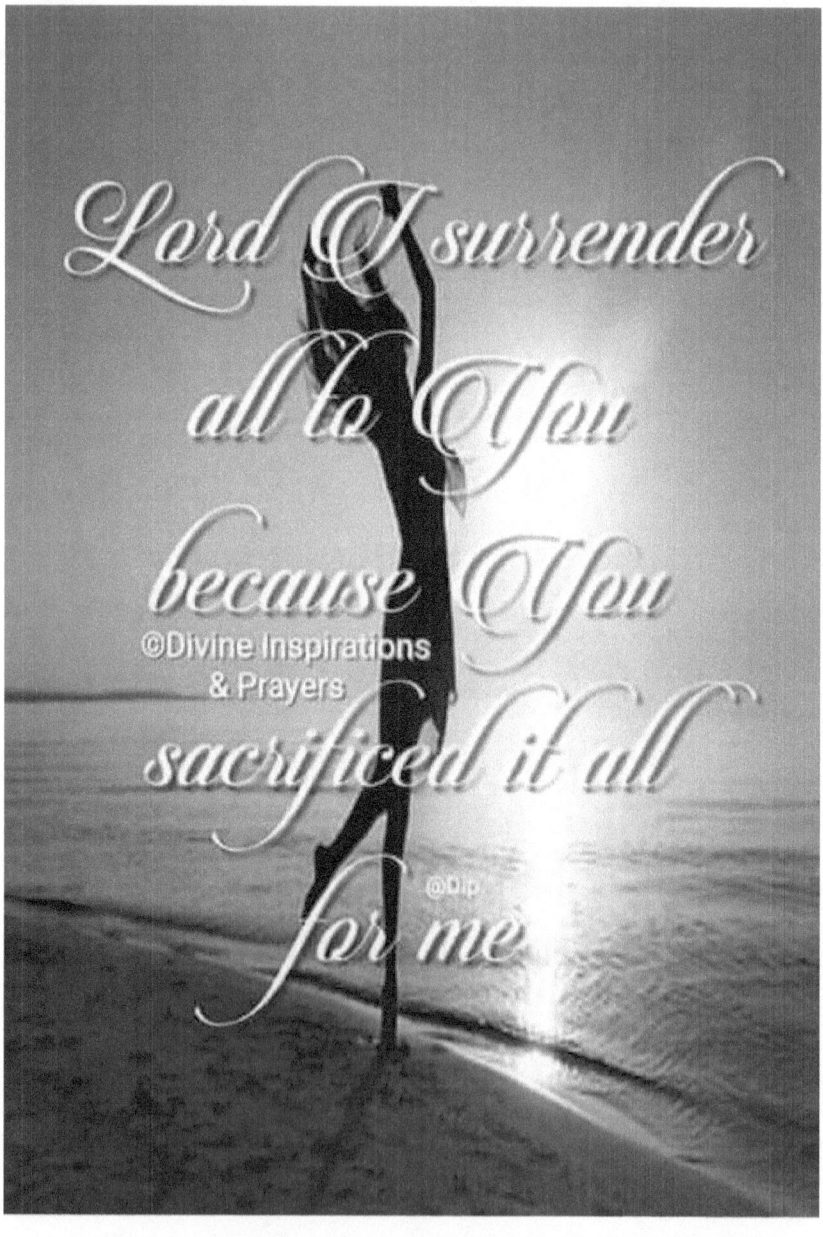

      Being played for a fool by some ideology or person and never achieving anything can't make you happy.

Not following the precepts set forth in the BIBLE is why you made JESUS cry. They are there to lead you to a loving destination. Your falseness and your ego will destroy you if you do not control your intake.

Greed is surely a main attribute in hate. Lust, envoy and control are other things that will deny your joy if you see them as you should. If you have been overtaken by them you may never notice it.
. You must choose it though and no matter where you are coming from – let go and let God into your life.

Do you really hope that you can SAVE AMERICA? If you are sincere you will advocate and enact GOD'S LAWS not your whims. If you hope to SAVE AMERICA the fundamentals must be secured and the foundation of AMERICA must be law.

Find some semblance of decency in life and focus on it. Achieve the positive for everyone – NOT JUST YOU.

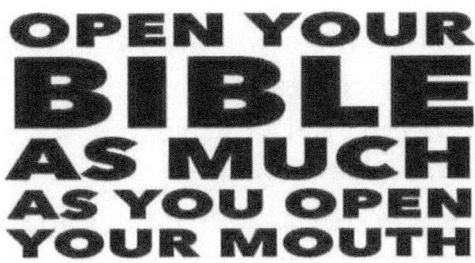

OPEN YOUR
BIBLE
AS MUCH
AS YOU OPEN
YOUR MOUTH

Guide with a firm, positive motion and help others achieve as well as you. It's all in how you approach life. Don't follow the insanity of greed, slovenly lust for power but aim for personal power that is meant for each of us in life.

You can be awesome if you choose to be in life. Those less fortunate always admire positive success. WHY NOT YOU?

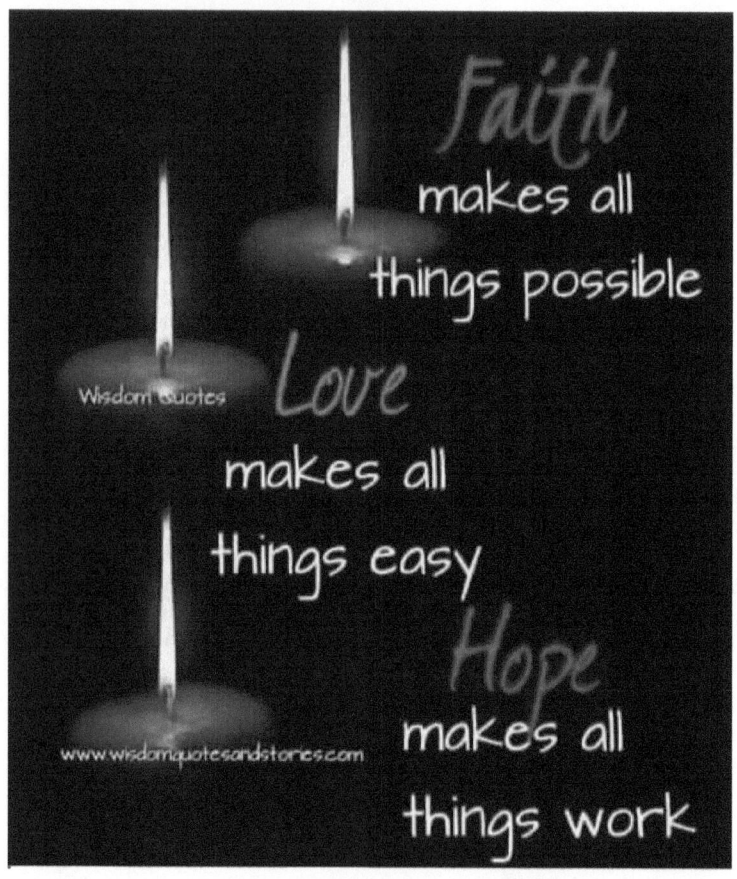

Faith makes all things possible

Wisdom Quotes

Love makes all things easy

www.wisdomquotesandstories.com

Hope makes all things work

Stop promoting the death mentality of abortion, infanticide, murder, genocide and react to it in a positive fashion. THOU SHALL NOT KILL is a commandment. One of God's laws in all Christian religions. Stop playing two ends against the middle. You can't be Christian if you support abortion. ABORTION is not HEALTHCARE. It's personal dignity that you need to assume. Actions speak louder then words and it doesn't take a rocket scientist to see what the HATERS want in life.

Decide what life holds for you and go after it. What is your passion can help round out what AMERICA needs as an integral component to be a success in life. Make good choices for yourself. Don't limit yourself.

When you condone what is obviously against God's law and accept other forms how can you expect anything positive? THOU SHALL NOT HAVE FALSE GOD'S BEFORE ME.

So if you shouldn't have any God's before the Heavenly Father, why is everyone so scared to stand up for him and not accept other religions who espouse HATE?

The BIBLE is the only word of God you should hold onto in life. RELIGION WILL NOT SAVE YOU ONLY JESUS CHRIST. Jesus is the only way to get into HEAVEN but you must accept him.

You can't dance with the devil and be with the Lord Jesus Christ at the same time. Obey his commandments if you Love Jesus. Jesus knows a fake and those who are frauds.

Be true to yourself. Stand up for God's will and things will go right for you. It's OK to make mistakes – everyone does. God forgives but expects you to repent and live the way you should.

This culture now of anything works is not acceptable to the Lord in any way. You see the signs of the Lord's distress – wars, fires, disasters everywhere. Read the BIBLE more then you talk and absorb the contents therein.

If you expect your life to be perfect you will end up disappointed. If you gloat there's disaster waiting. Be positive, be humble and do what is right.

"LEARN TO RESPECT"

The problem today, is everyone is afraid to respect because it's not politically correct. The word respect has no meaning to anyone any longer, because of the lack of values in life.

It makes no difference who you are each one of us is created equal. If you are a gazillionaire, a triple PhD holder, blue collar worker, homeless or any other form of title; it's not going with you when you die. ACHIEVE your title on earth as respecting all life, from birth to natural death and pray for all those who have had abortions, murdered in haste or any other issues. Love one another. Give hope to one another. Share your success with others and reap the joy of passing on your chain of love to others. That's respect.

If you see someone hurting – do something positive. Put God back into your day and end it with God. Aim for the positive always and let others see your joy. Spread it wherever you can.

When you go to school – say something nice to someone who has a sad face. Act as if it were you – what would you want others to do? RESPECT has to be learned, nurtured and become a natural. It starts with being taught, tried and tested. Yes, parents have the responsibility to raise children.

If you know someone in school is in a bad

way, let someone know and befriend them, don't bully them. Support the less fortunate – it could be YOU on the other side one day.

It's hard going to school these days and succeeding. There's so many elements that can drive a child to any angle in life.

Respect comes from the visual at times. If you approach life at a young age and teach hands on kindness, you find a support/mentor/coach WHO is not threatening but compassionate you can rub love in and help situations.

There have been several I've helped refocus, retrain and renew themselves and it's a successful approach. I am the type of person who feels that an immediate certified caretaker is scary and goes about issues in a certifiable method – whereas if you take the first step to a support/mentor/coach guide with the method of being the first step to medical professional care – you can discover more and get to the sourse of the issues at hand.

EXAMPLE: SUICIDAL people do not like to feel threatened because that can go negatively or positively. RESPECT issues everyone has them is my approach. I am here to hear you and guide you not the person who will medicate or lock you up. Once you discover the bond of trust the respect will automatically come into the situation.

Respect is attained with trust and we as a society must stop the hate, greed, lust and me first. We are all one in Christ Jesus and if we do not achieve the positive norms in life – there's no way anyone will SAVE AMERICA or themselves.

Realize the joy in learning from others and be thankful if its something positive. Never absorb negative if you want success in your life. I know it is hard to do and I struggle with this daily, but; if you want to live a Godly existence you must let go of everything, seek forgiveness and be forgiving no matter the pain. Much of the hurt in my life has gone, but still the betrayal is hard to take, especially due to it being family. God has it and I am now able to tolerate it more easily.

It makes no difference where the hate comes from – do not harbor it because it will infect your soul.

It's hard to believe that the greed in society can control behavior like ANTIFA, INFANTICIDE, HATE GROUPS and shootings, but it does. Are you happy if you earn some money to hurt people? Imagine if it was you on the other end and you were being hurt. Can you honestly justify hate? Is money more important to you then doing the right thing?

If you sit and evaluate yourself and what it will take for you to get RESPECT from others you will never receive RESPECT. Live like you own RESPECT and move to that beat. If you do, people who see how you treat yourself with respect and they will feel like it's not acceptable to mistreat you in any manner.

When you carry yourself with dignity and pride in yourself it shows real well. You will feel better, act better and have more incentive to do what's right and proper. Get out of the lazy hand out mode and achieve what you want for yourself.

This society is so me oriented and the democrat base wants to dominate. No human needs domination. We must all work to promote greatness and personal satisfaction in oneself. Seek HOPE, POSITIVE ACTION AND PEACE. Don't ever let anyone hold you back or control you.

PART OF RESPECT IS SUCCEEDING with self-confidence and motivation. Help everyone when you are able and watch life change.

If you have the Lord Jesus it is so much easier to respect and nurture life's goodness. Promote the positive in life and find ways to be inclusive. Don't look down on others – you don't sit higher then God, so; just assume its not your place to feel better then anyone else – just do the best with yourself.

I am so grateful that the hate filled in politics today does not overwhelm my soul.

The vitriol that the sorry losers seem to try to get by with in life will only end with their demise. Vengeance is mine says the Lord – if something does not wake them up God will.

The political games in D.C with such divisiveness and hate will render whatever God sees fit.

Class domination, status, egocentricity and machismo destroy hope. It is extremely nice that you can reach a level to feel superior because of intelligence, fortune or other means – but to much is given much is expected and that doesn't classify as anything more then what the least of God's people have attained in life.

Just consider that you may have had more opportunities handed to you in life. Let go of your ego because you're not taking it with you. So it is harder for others to advance for many reasons and you are not in any position to judge anyone. Be kind it won't hurt you.

What has boastfulness ever gotten you but a big head with nothing really of substance in it. Don't be like those who seek fame, fortune and worldly gifts, because; in the end it won't count at all. What you do with what you have is important if used correctly. If you use it for personal fame it will destroy you in the end.

Are you going to be a LEADER OR A FOLLOWER? Most followers don't seem to hold much respect. Look at those who have achieved the right things in life then follow that if you must. Why not be a LEADER? Stop allowing others to think for you. Don't fall for group thinking – you never know if it will kill you or produce what you want out of your life.

Respect doesn't qualify you for ignorance, danger or any action. Respect does help you appear more solid and informed.

There is something great in everyone. You may not see it visually but spend the time and find out in kindness and honesty. WHY not try and learn something new each day? Something positive that you can give a praise or shout out to whomever you learned it from.

Have the dignity to apply some common sense to your life and pass on all the good you receive. Start a chain of events that can help others and watch the respect, love and admiration exude out of you.

Respect the moments, the things you have and all that comes to you in life. Be open to the Lord and listen after you pray. SILENCE IS ALSO A PRAYER. Remember to allow yourself some silence. Be the best you that you can and rub confidence, hope and love in always. Forgive and let go.

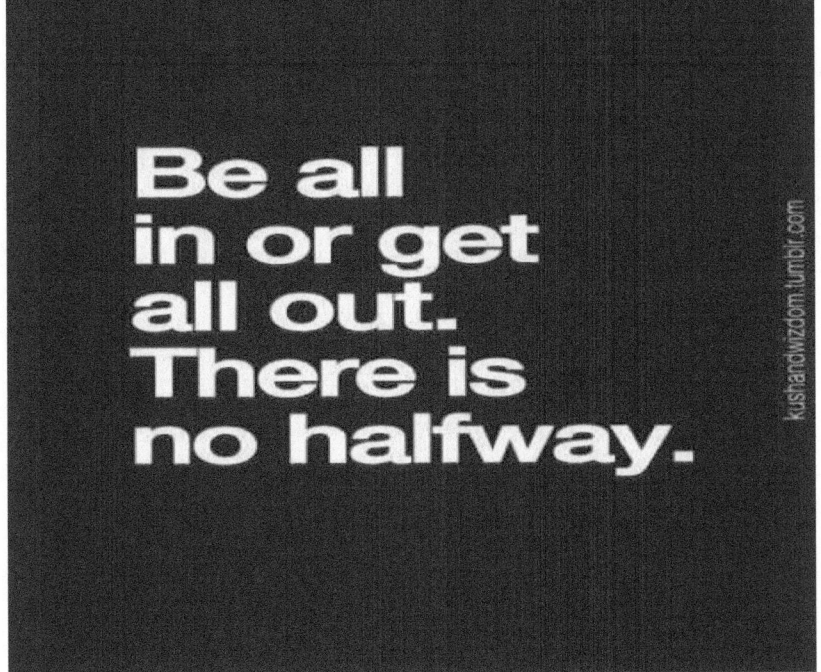

DO YOU THINK WITH THIS APPROACH YOU CAN HELP SAVE AMERICA? It makes no difference what happens in life as long as you are trying to achieve the best and be a good example to others. AMERICA was founded on sovereign nation with the principles and values that uphold Godliness. Learn all you can and love it. Try to be worthy of all those who have fought and died for your freedom.

You may not like or agree with things in life but if you face life with a broader view that things will go on, life will become more tolerable.

Help the young learn to be kind to one another and no bully. Help them to relish the diversity and culture of differences. Teach them how to share and become valuable citizens who cherish their blessings.

Be the light that shines in someone else's life and brings hope, love and everything positive. Make a difference in your world. Be a motivator not an excuse. Set an example for good behavior that can make a positive change in life. The young in school need to be taught not just educational knowledge, but life skills, survivor skills and a faith in one's one ability.

Do what you know is inherently right within you and care for others. Be a peacemaker not a gossiper. Help stop bullying in schools and rub RESPECT into those who are less fortunate. Your actions speak to the souls of those searching, needing and craving help. Silent pain is what brings negative out of people. Process for others a can do attitude and be supportive. Don't fall for what you hear fall for what is right as you feel within yourself.

Society wants everyone to be victims and group thinkers. God wants you to be victorious and self – motivated. What do you want for yourself? Are you a listener or a doer?

If you want to SAVE AMERICA, the rule

of law and Christian-Judaeo principles then you must study what they are, lean only on them and TRUST YOURSELF. Help and see what you can do to be positive in life.

Put a sparkle in someone's life that has no way of achieving it without you and love yourself. Never be satisfied with inaction or selflessness. Let your wings take you to wherever you need to help.

Don't be impressed ever – be excited for success for others. GOD SHOULD BE THE ONLY ONE TO IMPRESS YOU.

You have the ability to shape your life, you just have to make the right moves and never look back. Why not be a positive force for the good of everyone now?

Don't get stuck in the mud. Don't let anything hold you back. Work for the betterment of yourself, your surrounding areas and achieve all your meant to achieve in life.

Figure out the motion you must take and always be proactive.

Save yourself a lot of anxiety in life, by doing the right thing and never be opinionated. Everyone has their right to be as they are as long as it doesn't infringe upon anyone else. Choices have consequences and you need to be able to live with your choice.

Let go of all that's holding you back from all you have to offer the world. Use your talents to edify not detract in any manner. Be the leader you were meant to be and help others along the way. .

Put Jesus Christ back into life and teach it to others. Be that wonder that all are looking for in life and share the love.

When you strive for greatness don't be FAKE. When you achieve a victory in life – don't be egocentric and forget how you got it. Give praise to God out loud and invite others to as well.

SAVING AMERICA will take each one of us one step at a time to master what is the TRUE GLORY THAT AMERICA HOLDS FOR EACH OF US.
We must each find the love within ourselves to respect ourselves and pass it on regardless of any issue. We must seek others glory and be happy once they receive it and continue the positive actions of thankfulness, gratitude, appreciation, kindness, hard work, selfless efforts and respect the values of a Christian-Judaeo life. Appreciate sacrifices made and offered with humility and grace.

Never set the standard expected to high that you can not realistically achieve it in life. Always reach for more then less and never count on humans to be your supply chain. Adopt the attitude that I will do my best and if anyone can help along the way I will accept it and pass onto others what I can but; if no one will help me it's OK.

This is your life and your time to shine. Do it with all your might. Be an example of goodness. Let go of all that holds you back and SAVE AMERICA,

SAVE YOURSELF AND OTHERS TOO.

Yes, life is not perfect or exactly ever the way you wish, but with constant attention and work you can achieve what you need in life. You may never get everything that you want, but remember that there may be a reason why.

Just strive to be your best in life and exude the positive. You never know when you will draw your last breathe. Let your kindness, your success be the guide for others and always exude love. .

See the good in things and draw it out. Let the negative go and build on the positive good. BE AN EXAMPLE NOT AN EXCUSE.

If you really want to Save America and yourself you must refocus your mind now on only what is positive for you in life and pass it on.

REMEMBER THERE IS GREATNESS WITHIN EVERYONE.

IF you want to succeed in life badly enough you will. There's no such thing as can't. IT'S A MINDSET! RETRAIN YOUR BRAIN.

FEEL it in your heart and change what you need to in life. GET your life in order now and pass it on. https://www.youtube.com/watch?v=W6T_qoVoU5U Change and be strong. Listen to this video – KING FACE this video is awesome. ALL LIVES MATTER. No matter who you are in life YOU MATTER AND ARE LOVED BY YOUR CREATOR – THE HEAVENLY FATHER. It makes no difference if you are on death row, an abuser, a criminal of any kind – to God it doesn't matter. SINCERELY seek to repent, FORGIVE all those who've harmed you and forgive yourself and surrender your life to God now. . God's love is unconditional, limiting and seeking your love in return. Try God and know you are in the best arms possible. God will never turn you away. Your heavenly father sent his only begotten son to regain salvation for you. That's how much he loves you.

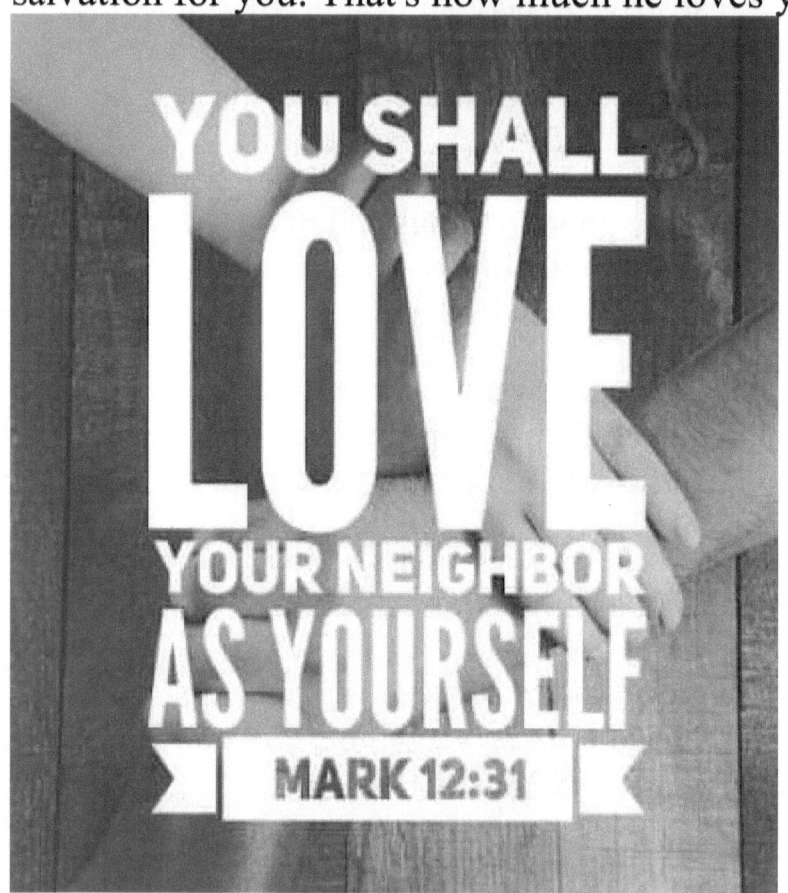

Yes, Jesus knows what you are going through, but; have you chosen him? Have you surrendered all of you to him yet? Being on Jesus's team is a choice you were born with and only you can make that choice. Jesus loves you no matter where you are in life. COME TO JESUS NOW.

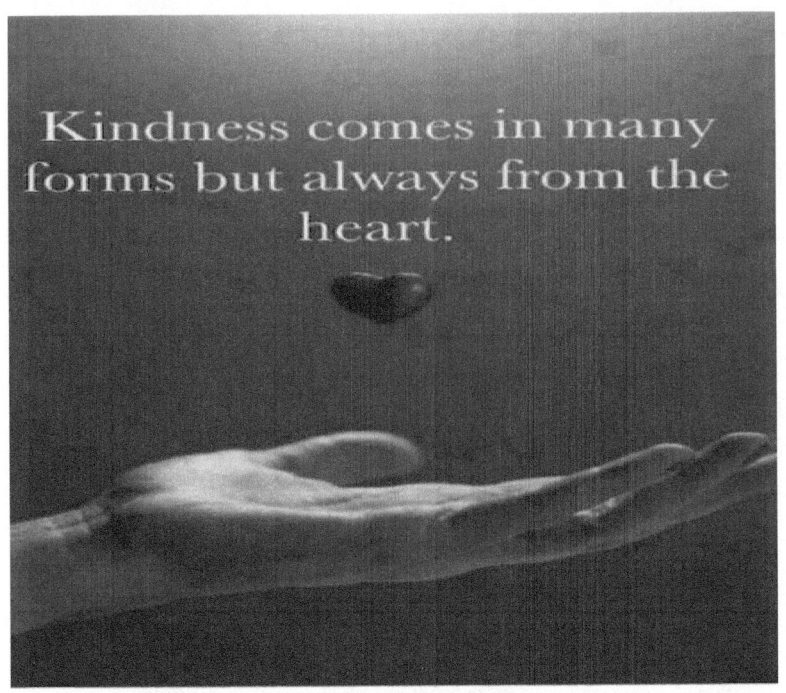

Kindness comes in many forms but always from the heart.

REMEMBER we all as humans do things in life that we are not proud of but; we are always forgiven and eternally blessed by God.

So if you've had ABORTIONS when you were young or whenever and now you've come to see the light of what your action really were – repent, respect yourself, forgive and live for Jesus.

So if you were in a GANG or were violent remember Jesus's disciples were evil too. There's no limiting with God's love. SEEK IT, LIVE IT AND PASS IT ON.

If you seek the right in life and beg God to enter your life, he will always forgive you and lead you.

Can you imagine everyone on earth being perfect? If we were why is there so much hate? WE are not meant to be perfect – we are meant to be great.

"REFOCUS AND ELIMINATE!"

**Beware
of the heartless,
who make your
heart beat quickly.
They're just using
your heart,
because theirs
won't start.**

AUTHOR
RACHEL HOLCHIN

Sure, nothing in life is easy but; it can be attained with retraining your mind and accepting yourself as a person who longs to be great. Help others achieve that too.

No one is truly in God's eyes any better then anyone else. We are all God's children and as a family of God we should strive to uphold the beauty in everyone. The homeless, the marginalized, the abused, the forgotten, the less fortunate etc can all improve themselves. WHY NOT BE A DOER NOT A RECEIVER?

Why not do it now and see the reaction? Work together with God and help all your brothers and sisters attain greatness. They all seek it no matter what they say but circumstances may need to change to acquire it. Remember, peoples lives ebb and they never remain the same. Remember the ocean waves they continually move at different speeds. Times change as well so; we as humans must become adaptable and react to the needs.

There's a reason why God says no to judge others and it's because for everyone issues vary. You are you and they are themselves. Be a positive not a negative and be proactive in all you do.

To those that much is given, much is expected. Just figure that you've been given so much that you can never stop helping and OVER HELP if you can. Make your efforts become a movement and cycle your actions in a positive way.

Give the gift of hope to someone you see that can use it. Hope is the fuel to ignite the drive in a person. Trust is the letting go and action that needs the fuel of hope to achieve the goals. They too have dreams and their goals. They too long for a future that is worthwhile and honest, but; circumstances forbid most of God's beloved to face life moment by moment with caution and care. You can be the HOPE to anyone if you wish to be in life.

If we all as a human being can grasp only personal issues and never expand on greatness, nothing will be achieved.

Let the fuel be ignited within you to give anyone you see the hope that they crave themselves. That's being a Christian not a hypocrite. Focus on eliminating all that is not honest within you and rub it in with love to all you meet.

See the joy and contentment you create in all those you lend hope to and feel the love you exude. Nothing can stop a ball rolling if its meant to roll unless it hits a dead end. Never stop repeating the good that you do, because the more you do the more you will receive.

JESUS IS COMING! BY: DAVID WILKERSON! https://www.youtube.com/watch?v=z0LWi17KwBI&feature=youtu.be&fbclid=IwAR1ILY_ogye0RyjRHuF7MJg49Qb0HFA2Kq1R1SND_dnROPVwk1ajEKNp2Fo

Strike a happy pace and generate as much force for the good of everyone and help exemplify the great character you were born with in life. We all are born with choice and options – release and refocus. Become a warrior for good.

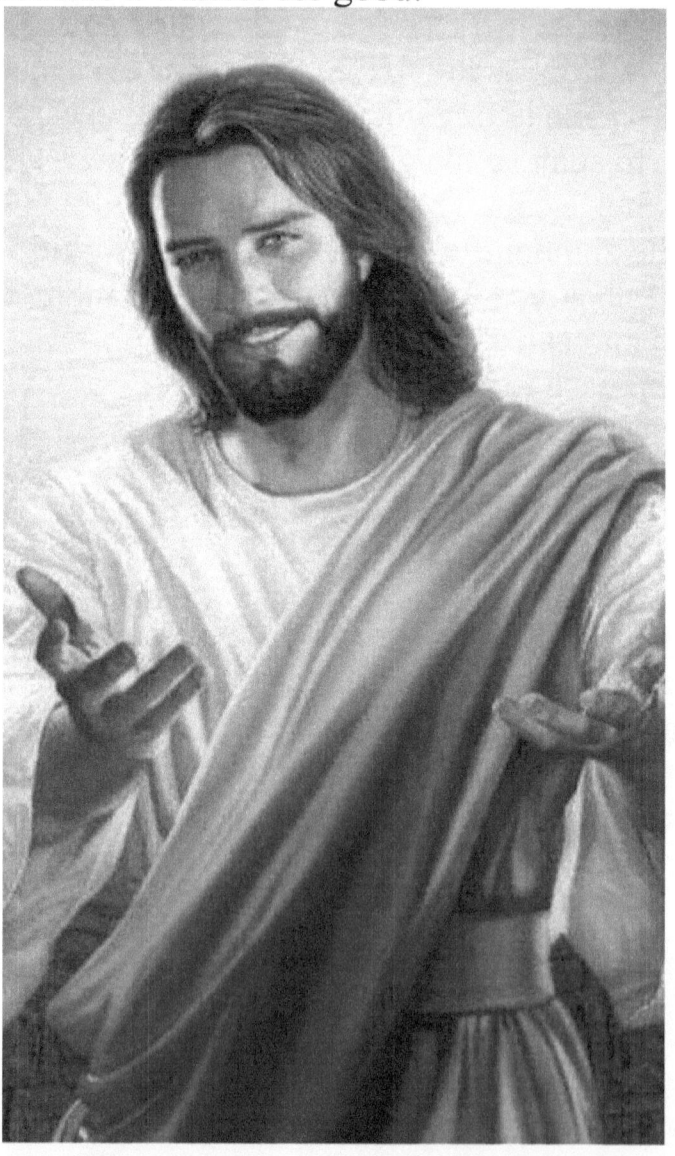

You are not defined by your mistakes. You are defined by God. He loves you no matter what. Romans 8:38

Achieve things and master them. Make them become second nature to you now and form a habit. It makes no difference if you are popular or being criticized for all you do. You do not have the time to waste on the insignificant elements of life. Try to be a part of the communities where you are familiar with and have the most impact. Learn the strengths and weaknesses and capitalize on having everyone succeed. Make people proud of their success, help them acquire positive elements and pass on the good.

No one has the same traits so it will be a great endeavor to blend talents to make them not have a reason to revert to old negative tendencies. REMEMBER, the devil is always going to attack those who are successful with temptations and be on guard. Stay committed to the Godly good things in life. REFOCUS yourself until the negative has no affect on you.

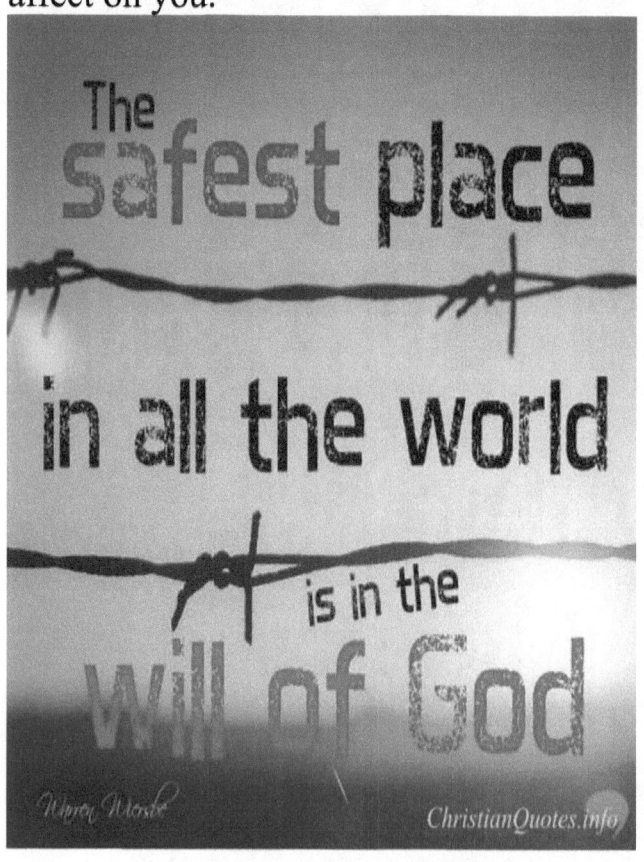

The safest place in all the world is in the will of God

ChristianQuotes.info

You have to believe that God hears you, loves you and trust in only him if you want him to act in your life. CHOOSE JESUS CHRIST NOW and live for him solely. Believe me, it's the best choice you will ever make in your life.

I am not saying he will make your life perfect I am saying he will guide you. Never expect anything – nothing is owed to you just because you are alive. Achieve your goals and master your journey so that in the end you can say, "Yes Lord I've done my best with what I had."

You have to seek the Lord and your best because only you know what it is and God. Lead yourself to a happen goal and pass it on.

If you are always searching and never finding things and figuring things out in life, you need to make a change. Stop seeking worldly fame and seek God and all else shall come to you.

If you're seeking worldly fame and fortunate, you may risk missing out on your eternal glory. Why not do what you know in your heart is right and meant for you?

If you aren't sure of yourself and the path you want to take let God guide you. Be still and know that he is Lord. Listen after you pray. Wait until you are sure you hear God and hold on tight. Greatness starts with a positive mind.

It's hard to remain positive all the time, but if you want to beat SATAN and all the negative in the world you must fight for yourself, trust yourself, love yourself and achieve your goals.

God knows what you need. You need to figure out what you need and let go. YOU HAVE GOD'S DNA within you – beautify yourself.

You hold the awesomeness of being great

which you were created with inside you, but; it's your choice to use it. Why not try a new way of doing things and see yourself soar? Be always mindful of others and how you can reach out. Feel the greatness within yourself and produce the fuel to ignite others.

You are a fabulous creation, a magnificent formation which God fore-ordained and will lead you – just let go.

Always seek forgiveness and forgive and move on. God will never leave you if you fully commit to him. There will be times that are terrible but; you must walk through the darkness to get to the light. .

Don't expect a handout or a guide dog, just do it yourself and be proud of accomplishing your own success truly for yourself.

If you are waiting for a handout make sure its appropriate for you or you will fail. God knows what you need and will give it to you if you trust. LET GO!

You must walk your journey and choose Jesus because no one goes to the Father unless you choose Jesus Christ first.

Let your light shine with the LOVE of the Lord and the path become truly yours. Let Jesus lead you.

It's a choice you must make and you must know it within yourself – no one can force it upon you and Jesus does not want you to choose him and not be a real follower. Follow the source of eternal love now.

No one said that your life would be perfect and no one owes you anything. You are alive due to your parents and you need to focus only on your greatness and goals. Why delude yourself into thinking someone can do it for you? IT WILL END UP TO BE A LOSING BATTLE IF YOU DO.

If you don't trust yourself to succeed why should anyone else care? RESPECT YOURSELF and achieve your goals. Give the glory to God and keep moving on.

Just like the ocean the currents change all the time. So do the currents in your life. No matter where you are or where you start – just start and hang on to the hope of achievement AND RESPECT of yourself. Always think for yourself and make sure you are content with your choice and that you can accept the consequences. Be willing to fail if you must in order to attempt to change and achieve your goals. Never accept giving up or letting go of anything important to you in life. JUST walk your walk and always get up and start over if you must. Mistakes in life happen and you can learn by them.

Try your best and pass it on. Make life the best you can for everyone you meet. Even if you feel like hell someone else feels worse then you. Be the light that changes someone's life. Remember others hurt, others live and feel and you can make a difference with a smile and a prayer.

Be your BEST always even when you don't feel like it and remain positive. Good things will naturally happen if you do. Remain positive. Live to be an asset to others. Be an example not an excuse.

Never follow anyone – because you really

don't know where they are going in life of if the destination is beneficial or not.

Make the most of yourself. It makes no difference what you lack or have we all are DIFFERENT and have greatness within ourselves. Don't fall for the negative STAND FOR THE POSITIVE IN LIFE. So many people do not care anymore and have only their self interests at heart. You must be the only one to control your existence and never permit yourself to be lead. YOU ARE YOUR OWN LEADER – LISTEN TO YOUR HEART and go with it always. Don't seek acceptance, approval or popularity in anything. If it's right for you that should be good enough. God wants your best.

Why not give success a chance and let go? It's a chance for you to feel good and promote the best things in life. It's your choice. It's your way. It's greatness at it's best. You can achieve it if you let yourself. What are you waiting for? Don't count on anyone to achieve it for you because it won't happen.

Human beings are motivated for their own success and have human flaws. Don't let others control what you can accomplish in life. Don't let main stream establish what you do in life. Walk your own path to success and help OTHERS receive.

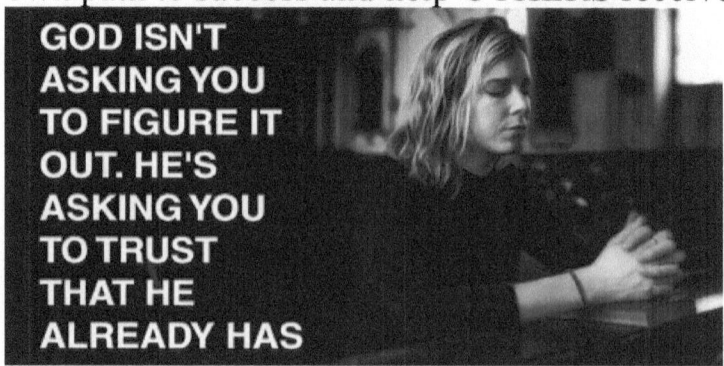

GOD ISN'T ASKING YOU TO FIGURE IT OUT. HE'S ASKING YOU TO TRUST THAT HE ALREADY HAS

You may not get many chances in life to change the pattern or sequence of your life. Just do it and trust. Life is not unending and you know not when he is coming so; DO IT NOW!

With society as torn as it is politically just focus and renew what you need. There's no telling what the future will be or how it will turn out. Depend on yourself and the greatness within you and thrive now.

Master what you must. Master what you can. Master your inner being the best that you can. Strive to succeed and be all you can be in life.

YOUR DESTINY IS UP TO YOU SOLELY. DESIGN IT YOUR WAY ONLY.

Don't succumb to mediocrity or self-indulgence reach out and try a new angle if you must. Surround yourself with hope and loving people and let go of your past. It's hard sometimes to relinquish it all and maybe it's not meant to be let go. Sometimes through prayer, intense commitment and renewal you can achieve a semblance of Godliness in your life. Just never expect anything in life to be perfect. Live to be honest, positive and an achiever always. Let go of everything else.

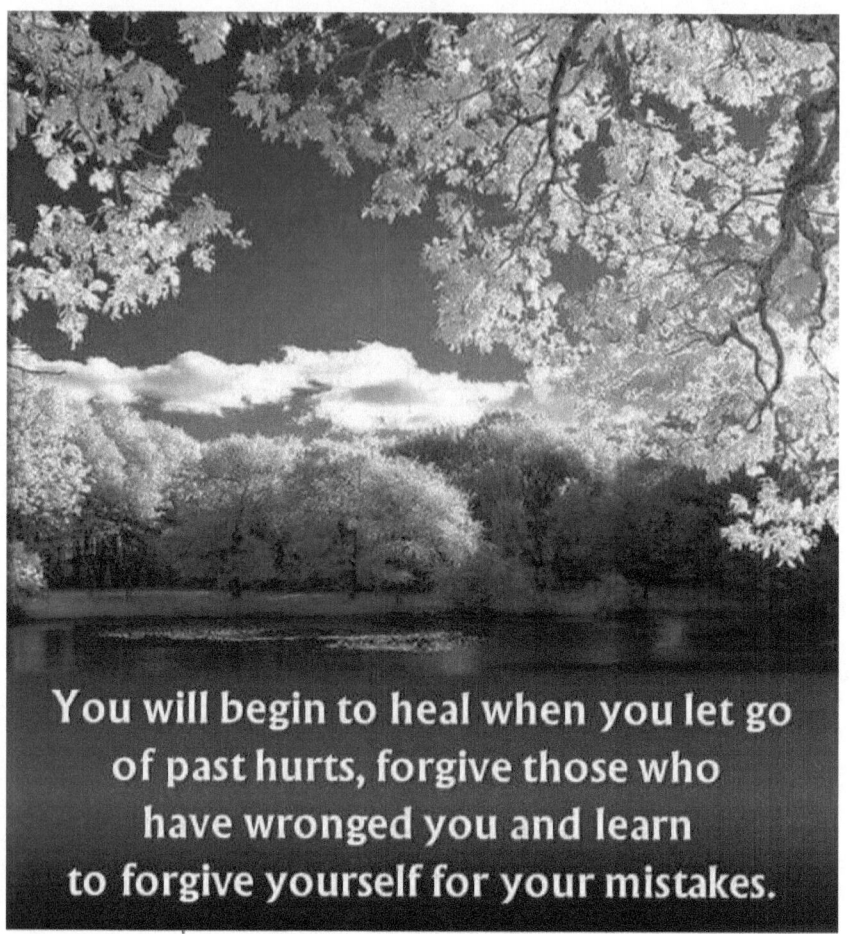

You will begin to heal when you let go
of past hurts, forgive those who
have wronged you and learn
to forgive yourself for your mistakes.

Only in positive honest action can you truly move in the right direction. You can not control what others do – but you can help them choose – do not sugar coat anything because; ultimately the truth comes out.

Please put prayer into your life and pray incessantly. Prayers do get answered and it's your communication with God. He loves to hear you call on him. It makes him happy and loves your attention. Please never get upset with your prayers never being answered or never on your time. REMEMBER God's time is not our time and if you do not receive what you pray for, maybe God has something much better in mind for you..

God sees and knows what we need and can do miracles as well, so; pin your hopes and sights on that.

No matter who is PRESIDENT – GOD is always going to be victorious.

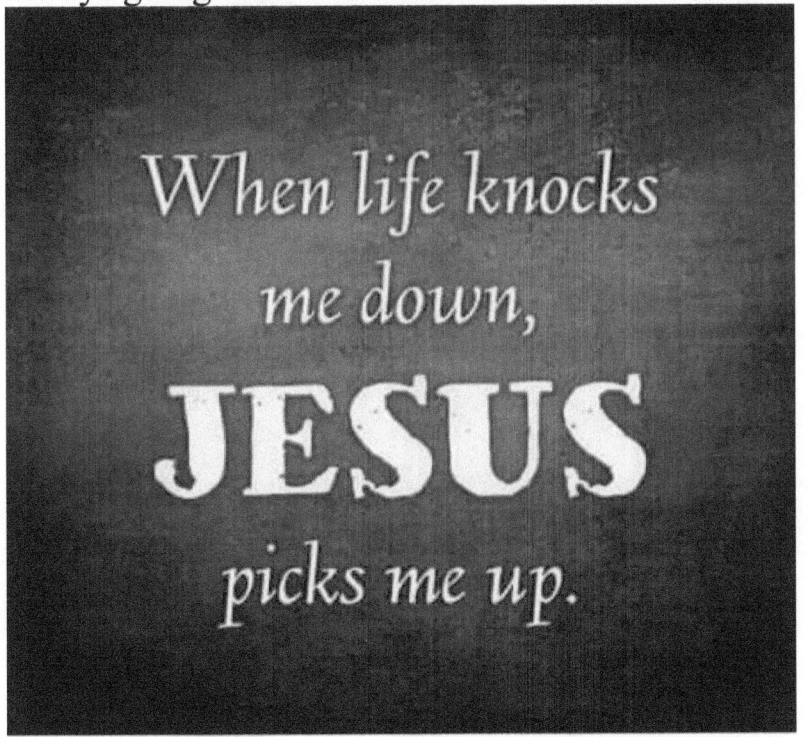

When life knocks me down, JESUS picks me up.

You are on a journey – as we all are now and how your journey turns out is up to you. Don't be a follower. Only follow your heart after you've thought about your actions. Pray and move forward.

Find that happy median and strive always to remain within it. No matter what your past has been you must realize we all have one. Just remain happy and positive and let no one suck the air out of you.

You can help you sustain yourself if you sincerely seek him and receive him. It's not a joke. You will live until you die and the choice is yours to make in life. Do you want to survive or just be alive?

Try trusting yourself enough to give yourself a chance. Never look back. You can't get it back and you can not redo the past. MOVE ON.

People will always have an opinion about you But you live your life for the Lord not people

It really is worth a shot to forget the past, forgive what's in the past and lead yourself into the light.

Gang members, murders, sex offenders, drug addicts, abusers whatever the label you put on yourself or let society place on you are forgiven, can BE AWESOME and will be with God if they choose HIM. Seek ye first the kingdom of God and all else shall come unto you.

Never let the power hungry destroy your goals in life. Never focus on too far ahead of you. Make success achievable with small decisive, deliberate motions and never look back.

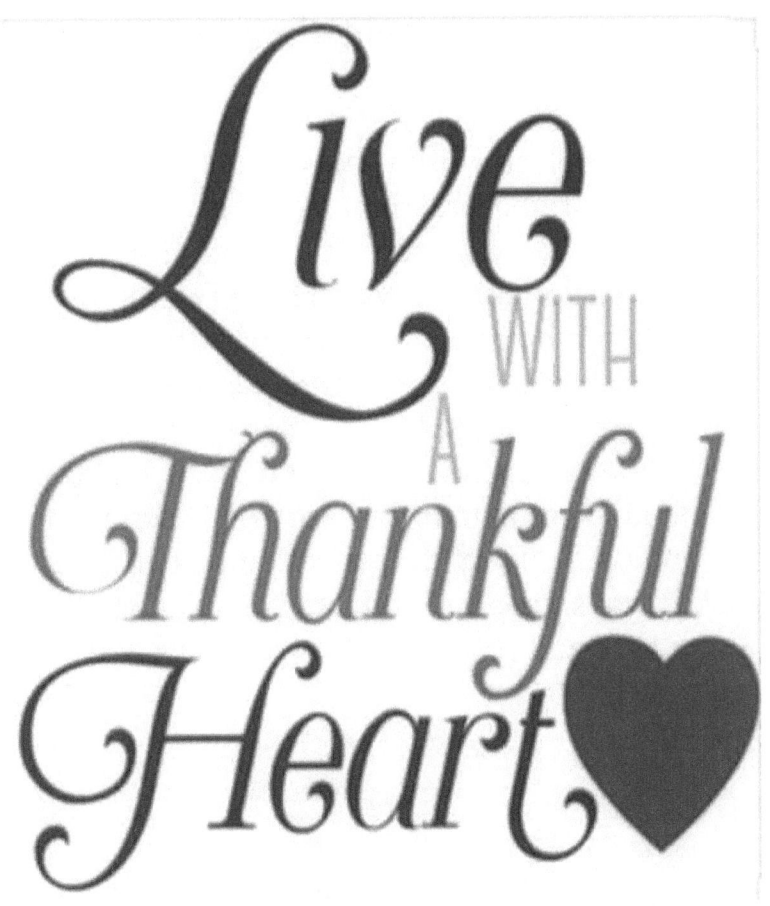

NO HUMAN IS BETTER THEN
ANYONE ELSE. WE ARE ALL GOD'S
CHILDREN! We are all on a journey and it's all you
have to focus on. STOP the needing to please others
and please yourself and GOD.

It's your time to cherish what God has
given you and what you are now. BEAUTIFY IT
NOW.

Walk yourself to a place in life that you can
be contented with and progress from there. Make little
improvements and dream. You can overcome what
you want if you let yourself fail, let yourself redo and
expect that you can achieve the best in life. Never
expect perfection because you will end up defeated all

the time. As long as you are alive be grateful and strive.

Your efforts are what will keep you motivated in the right direction. Never give up and never lose hope. You can make it through life with only Jesus to back you up if you TRUST completely. I have. Life should be good for everyone – but in life we have many obstacles and must never give up.

The Lord says, "seek ye first the kingdom of God and all else shall come unto you." Believe in yourself and God. No matter what you face in life. There are always people who have worse things then you. Share love and receive it. Never expect and you will never be let down.

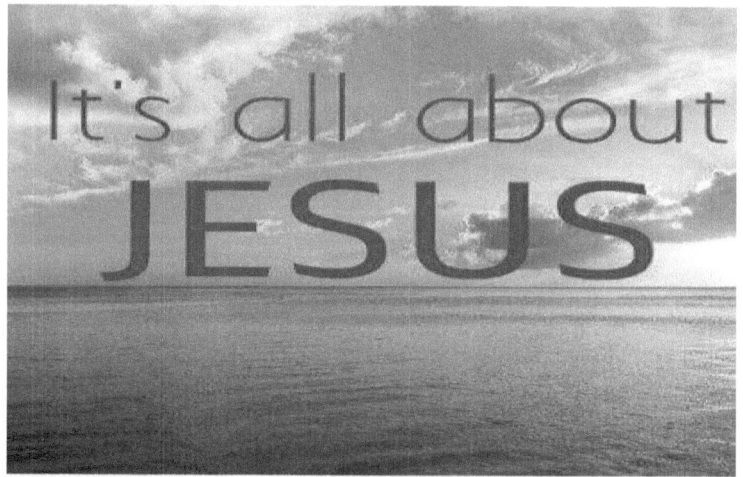

Live for what is right for you and your relationship with God. No one else's impression, opinion or comments should sway you in any way. I've learned that if it can not enhance your life it should not make a difference to me.

I have become resigned to the fact that I can only control what I can and God must do the rest. I am accountable only to what I do in life and truly hope I can guide others to their goals.

We all have different goals, but; there's usually a common thread to all of them. MASTERY. HOPE AND SUCCESS.

So many people hurt, so many people are selfish and beyond the normal reach to help. You must refocus and eliminate the things that are hanging on that are negative. EVEN a brother, sister or very distant genetic being. Put them all in God's hands now. RELEASE YOURSELF FROM ALL THINGS.

You aren't taking anything with you when your journey is over. Trust yourself enough to BE AWESOME and fulfill all your needs.

It may be a simple thing that you do, but; for someone else that gesture can be the pivotal point in their life. Be a CHRIST WARRIOR and pursue your goal with vengeance. Never leave anything undone. Pursue what is a passion for you and master it. Be the best you that you can and improve each day. Let others see your joy and pass it on.

"BELIEVE YOU CAN!"

Always be thankful no matter if you can't see a reason to be. You could have something someone else has which could be worse.

> **Sometimes the strongest among us are the ones who smile through silent pain, cry behind closed doors, and fight battles nobody knows about.**

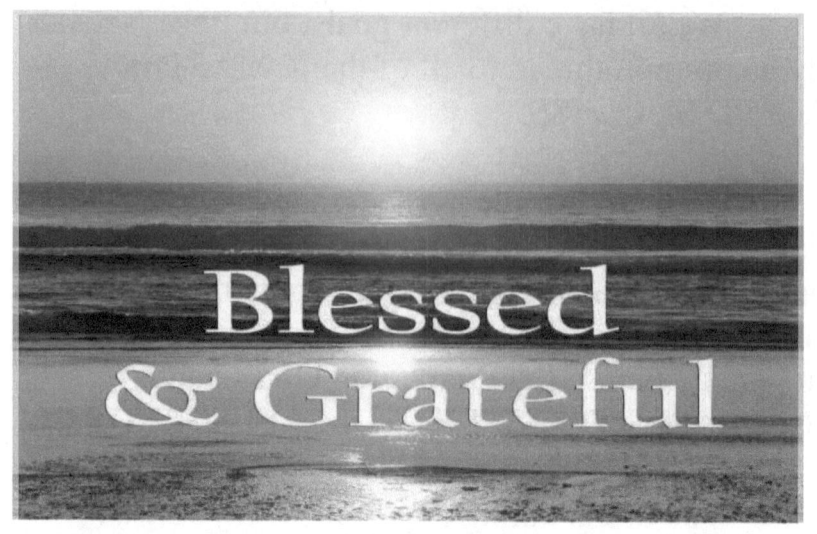
Blessed & Grateful

If you approach your life in a positive manner it most often times will be positive. DON'T let others discourage you. There are so many elements in life that cause people to want to give up, quit or even commit suicide. Face your issues head on and discard them one by one. The ruling class does not dictate what road you travel on – ONLY YOU.

You can take small steps and achieve great things over time. Master each step and move on. Look at what is being offered to you in life and don't succumb to anyone's philosophy but your own. Be true to yourself and seek honesty in life. Once you exude that view in others minds – respect will come.

Don't waste your time chasing worldly issues because you will miss the eternal issues. The more you look for pleasure and tangible worldly things you will never have enough time to focus on what really matters in the end.

SAVE YOURSELF! SAVE AMERICA! SAVE THE LIFE GOD SENT FOR ALL OF US.

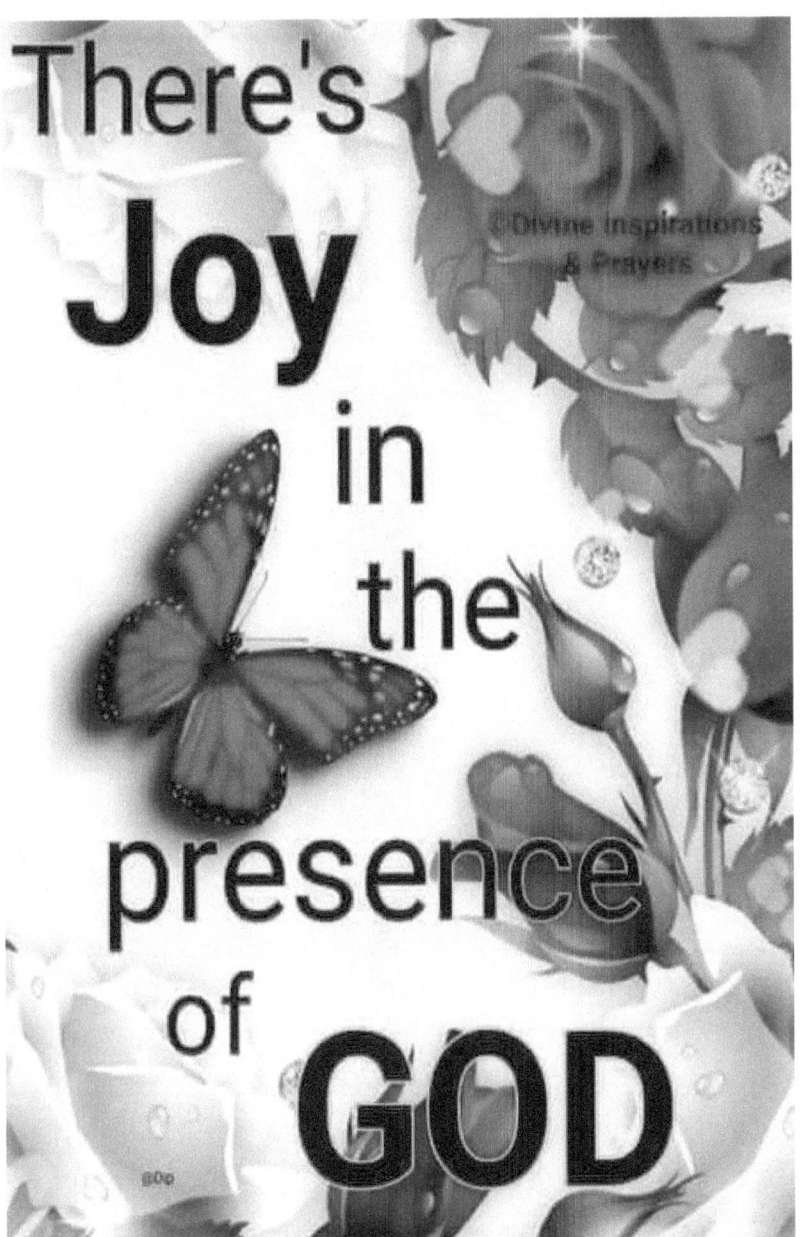

There's **Joy** in the presence of **GOD**

©Divine Inspirations & Prayers

Feel the joy of passing on real guidance and success.

You will never have what others have in life and there's no reason to strive for it. You aren't going to take things with you when you are called home – so why not focus on reality? Why not focus on making sure you achieve eternal life? IT'S A CHOICE WE ALL MUST MAKE.

The Spirit of
the Lord says,
"I'm putting you in a place
by Me where they will
be able to SEE you
but not REACH you"
Your enemy will only
be able to watch as I bless
you from every direction

PROPHET JEFF JANSEN

FORGET trying and be natural. FORGET impressing and be an example. In the end where is everything going to go. Do you think that what has cluttered your existence will help anyone else? Probably not. Succeed on your own terms. That way you will be sure that the goals you are trying to master are the one's YOU WANT. Lead yourself to success.

I know it's painful sometimes to have to do things all alone, but think of the joy you will receive in the end when you achieve your goals and have successfully won your destiny the way you hoped.

WHEN SOMEONE IS BROKEN, DON'T
TRY TO FIX THEM - (YOU CAN'T).
WHEN SOMEONE IS HURTING, DON'T ATTEMPT
TO TAKE AWAY THEIR PAIN - (YOU CAN'T).
INSTEAD, LOVE THEM BY WALKING BESIDE
THEM IN THE HURT - (YOU CAN).
BECAUSE SOMETIMES WHAT PEOPLE
NEED IS SIMPLY TO KNOW THEY
AREN'T ALONE. ALL-GREATQUOTES.COM

Your lifetime seems like it will last forever but; truly you never know how long it will be til God calls you home. Be grateful you have an opportunity to obtain your goals.

BELIEVE IN YOURSELF BECAUSE GOD BELIEVES IN YOU.

Give yourself a break and move on. You can't do anything about what others are doing around you so; do your thing. It's up to you to choose to be GREAT.

MAKE A DIFFERENCE NOW IN YOUR LIFE. There's no telling when JESUS is coming.

God is looking
for people
through whom
He can do
the impossible.
What a pity
we plan to do
only
the things
that we can do
by ourselves.

— A.W. Tozer

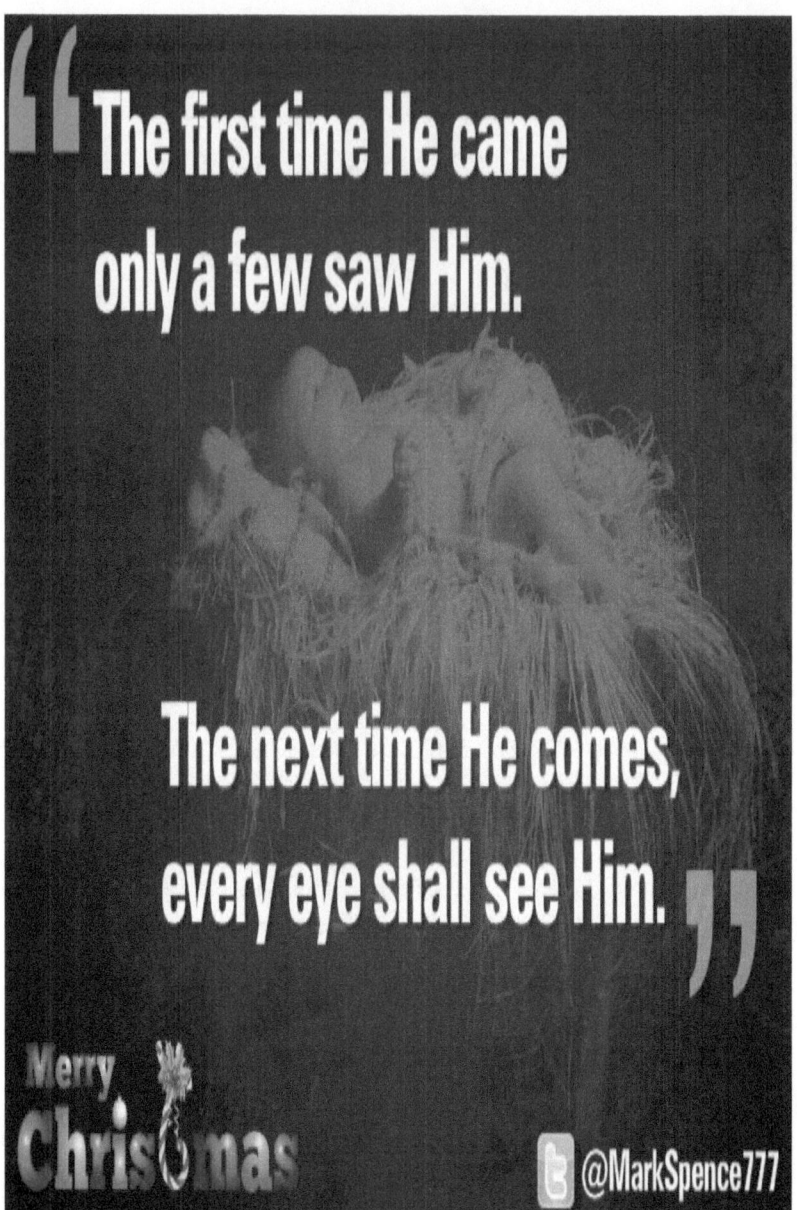

"The first time He came only a few saw Him.

The next time He comes, every eye shall see Him."

Merry Christmas

@MarkSpence777

Just start with trying to do something positive to help yourself and let others see you succeeding.

EXAMPLE – is a great motivator for anyone. When others see your success they may reach out and try for themselves. Wouldn't you be happy to think that someone tried because of you and may have a better life because of you.

JESUS SAID
I AM THE WAY THE TRUTH & THE LIFE
NO ONE COMES TO THE FATHER EXCEPT THROUGH ME

When you are doing the right things and feeling good – things will be happening regularly on a more positive note for you in life.

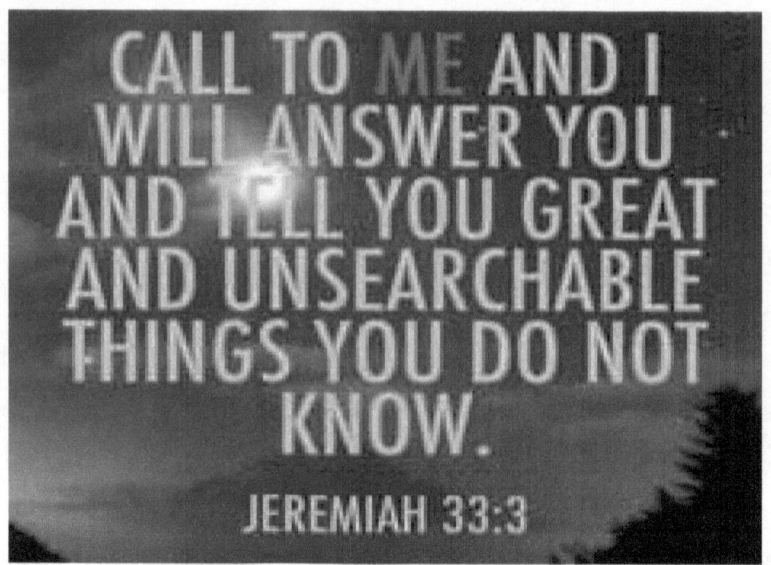

CALL TO ME AND I WILL ANSWER YOU AND TELL YOU GREAT AND UNSEARCHABLE THINGS YOU DO NOT KNOW.

JEREMIAH 33:3

Lead yourself in the right direction and you will succeed. Things will be more bearable and less stressed. Nothing in life will be perfect. You will always need or want more. That's part of our human nature. Accept what you are, what you have and amplify the best in you always. It makes no difference where you are in life. CONFUSE those who feel they are above you, ENHANCE those who are with you and ALWAYS BE POSITIVE.

Don't anticipate anything. Move to your own beat and make it through each day.

YOU CAN! IF I CAN!

If we all adopt an attitude of I CAN things can get better for each one of us. If we create a chain reaction AMERICA CAN be saved as well. If you want to it can happen. If we all strive to it will. EVERYONE NEEDS OPTIMISM IN LIFE. If there's a negative – it's not meant to be.

Wake up! Stand up! Remember the souls who have fought and died for this country since it was founded. Don't they deserve some GRATITUDE, RESPECT, HONOR and DIGNITY?

A – Absolutely
M – Master
E – Everything that's
R – Right with an
I CAN – Attitude!

If you are an American legal citizen you are an AMERICAN and it is up to you to choose your own destiny. You can succeed and you can believe in yourself staunchly enough to be your absolute best in life. Don't expect anything in life to be perfect, just be grateful you can make ends meet each day. Nothing is promised to you – just because you are born.

Decide for yourself to be an I CAN ATTITUDE – always be positive. CONFUSE those who are skeptical of you. SMILE always and make others see that you are happy. LEAD yourself to a place where others will want to follow. SUCCESS is different for everyone. Adopt the right attitude for

Some people aren't loyal to you, they are loyal to their need of you. Once their need changes, so does their loyalty.

yourself and let your life be your statement that you are alright with where you are no matter where anyone else is in life. See the chain reaction from the doubters in life and proceed to stimulate others minds.

Let others follow the right course in life and live decently. People don't naturally flock to negative situations and things. There are elements in life that happen and must be eliminated. I am still working hard on this myself. Panic and anxiety is the weakest part of me now.

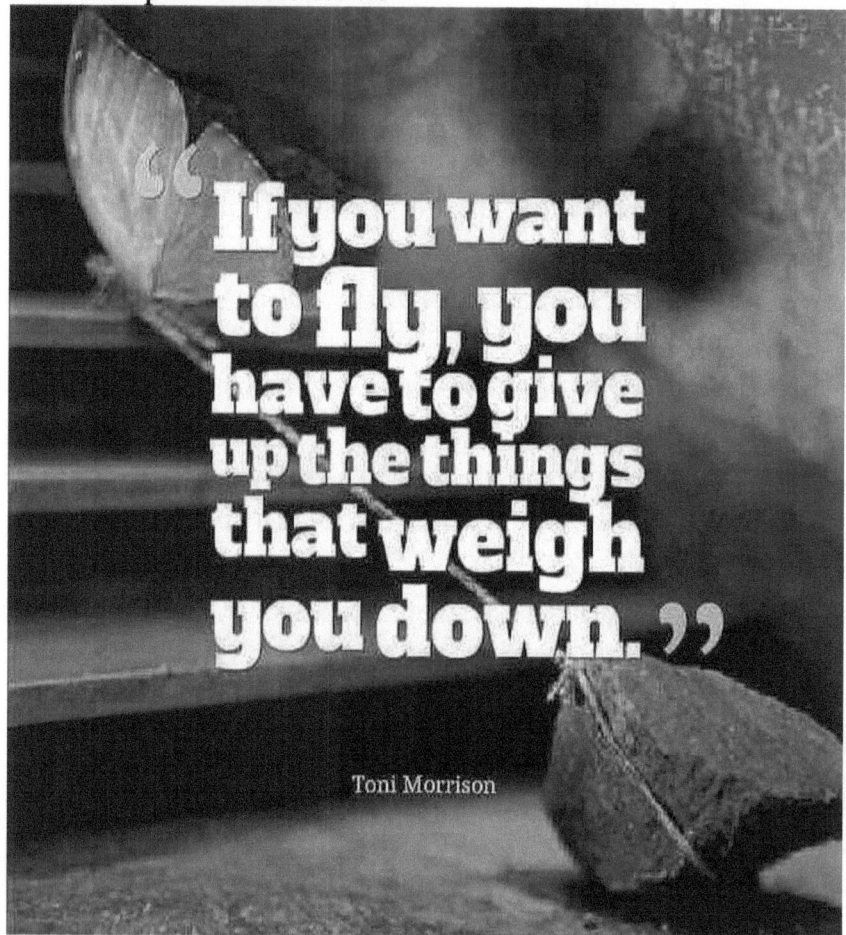

"If you want to fly, you have to give up the things that weigh you down."

Toni Morrison

Everyone seems to have issues they must encounter and discard in order to move on. I've always had to be the fall person and now there's no one but God and he's never let me down once. Only human beings have let me down. That's where the panic and anxiety rests. God is showing me a new view and teaching me to let go. Yes, I love to confuse people because in confusion you can see reality. If they think you're ok they leave you alone.

Be an I CAN and see for yourself. Sometimes it is truly fun, especially the one's who don't have your best interests at heart get unwrapped as FAKE and they get uncomfortable within their own surface. BE YOURSELF AND ACHIEVE. SMILE and let everyone think what they want and let go.

JESUS IS THE GIFT
*that perfectly fits
the size of every heart.*

Try to focus only on what's the best result for yourself in life and help others if they genuinely seek it. Stay away from the pseudo – gyms in life. PSEUDO'S are fake and can be contagious if you succumb to them.

Don't play games with anyone because those who do not have your best interests at heart always seek to in turmoil. Let go of all the stress and do whatever is right for you to do in life.

Sometimes God Will SLOW You Down So That The EVIL Ahead Of You Will PASS Before You Get There. Your DELAY Could Mean Your PROTECTION. HE'S A GOOD GOD!

It really is a hard lesson to learn in life. REMEMBER that not everyone has your best interests at heart. Pursue them on your own terms and expect nothing from anyone. Don't even worry about issues. Let God handle it all.

ONE FAKE FRIEND can do more damage to you the TWELVE haters who lust after your destruction.

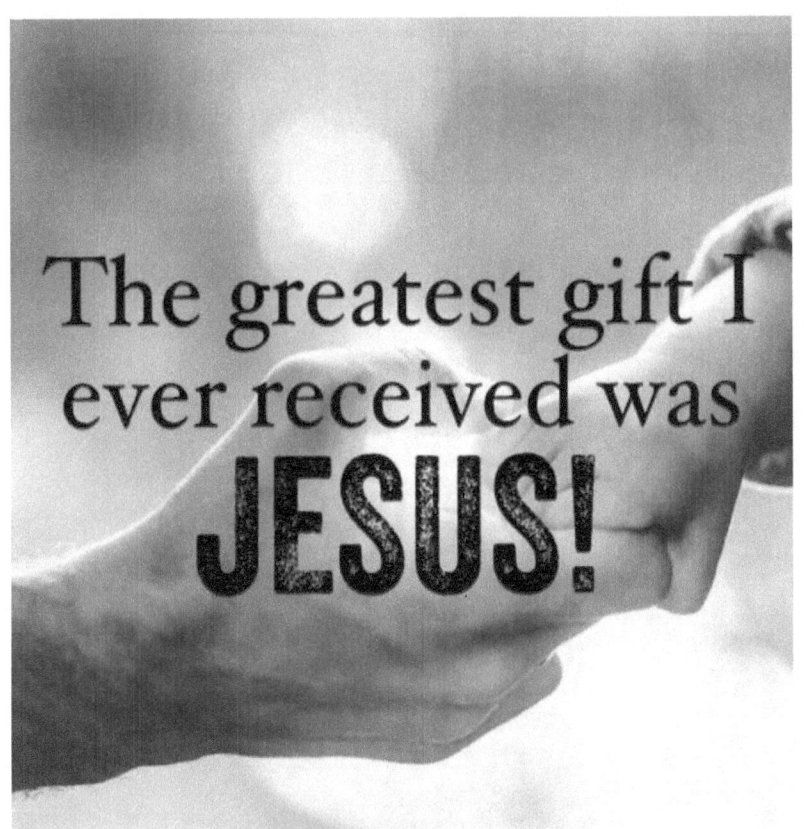

The greatest gift I
ever received was
JESUS!

       It really doesn't make a difference if you
are accepted or not by anyone. Jesus will accept you
no matter what and is the only RIGHT ANSWER.

       The worldly pursuits are superfluous for
you to pursue because they will never amount to
much.
Grasp onto only what can be totally positive in your
life. If it doesn't feel right it isn't right for you. Forgive
yourself and trust yourself to let go. I am struggling
with this and slowly learning that I have to love
myself enough to trust that what I crave will happen
the right way for me.

       Yes, only I can achieve it and I do believe I
can master what I must in life. I have been struggling
so hard to let go of my panic and anxiety and God's
love is working on it.

WHEN GOD WANTS TO MOVE YOU TO BIGGER BLESSINGS, HE'LL ALLOW A HEAVY STORM TO POUR ON YOU. EVERY PLANT GROWS AFTER RAIN. Stay confident, stay focused and realize your dreams. Water those good seeds and watch success arrive. Don't let anything discourage you or convince you to give up on yourself. Nothing controls you but you.

Please don't quit or give up. You are loved by God in a very special way. Remember – I am not perfect and you are not perfect and anyone who thinks they are, YOU'D BEST RUNAWAY from them fast. Nothing in life is suppose to be perfect – it's a journey to a destination where perfect unity, peace and eternity will reign.

Don't spend your time looking at the passed because you may miss what's waiting for you for the future. Work on what you feel can achieve your greatness and let go. I am truly trying to do this.

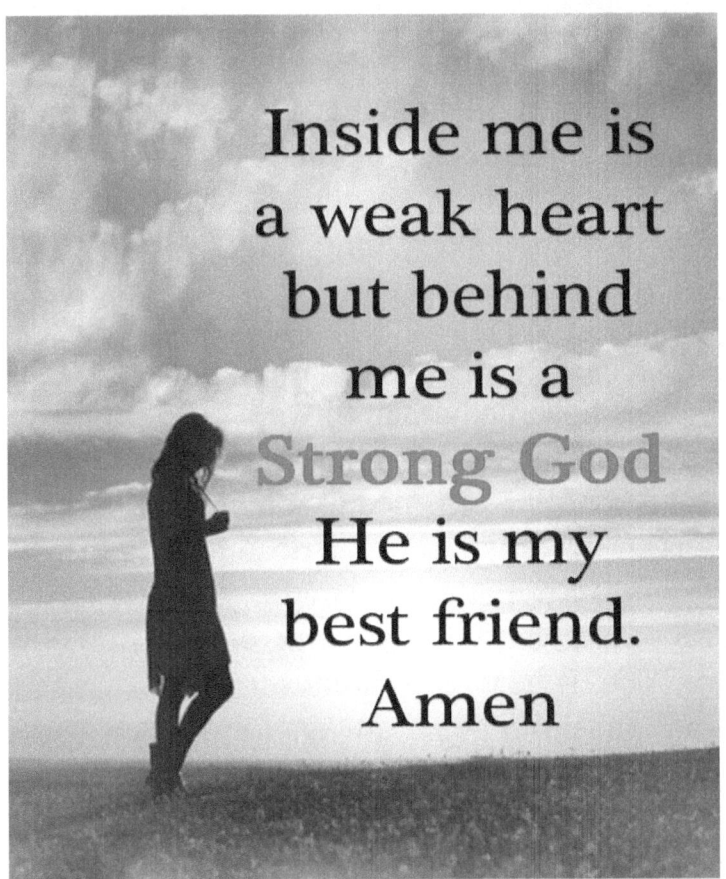

Inside me is
a weak heart
but behind
me is a
Strong God
He is my
best friend.
Amen

Lord I know my weak heart needs you every second of my day. I know you are the only reason why I am still alive. I have felt your forgiveness of all my sins through the sins in my life and the release felt within me. PLEASE always remember that I truly forgive everyone everything in my past and surrender this to your care LORD JESUS and pray that you will consume me fully.

WITH you oh Lord and your word the BIBLE I pray that my journey will be steadfast and guided only by you. RELEASE ME and release everything not meant for me. HOLD all in your loving embrace. Teach those in my past your ways oh Lord through your word the BIBLE.

FORGIVENESS, REPENTANCE &

ACCEPTANCE IS YOURS IF YOU CHOOSE IT.

Be an example not an excuse. Be an asset not a cop out. Live your best life and let everything go. You aren't meant to hold your trash you are meant to discard it and forgive everything daily. No one's opinion should matter because you aren't here to live for anyone but for GOD.

Jesus became human to walk our journey and become one of us. Jesus preached as a child to teach his father's will. Jesus died as a man to save us from our sins. Jesus arose from the dead now to bring us all back home. No matter how awful your life has been GOD'S will is that you seek him, choose him and live for him. YOUR heavenly father's love is unconditional, unlimiting and always forgiving.

BE AWESOME – achieve the best you can in life and help others to as well.

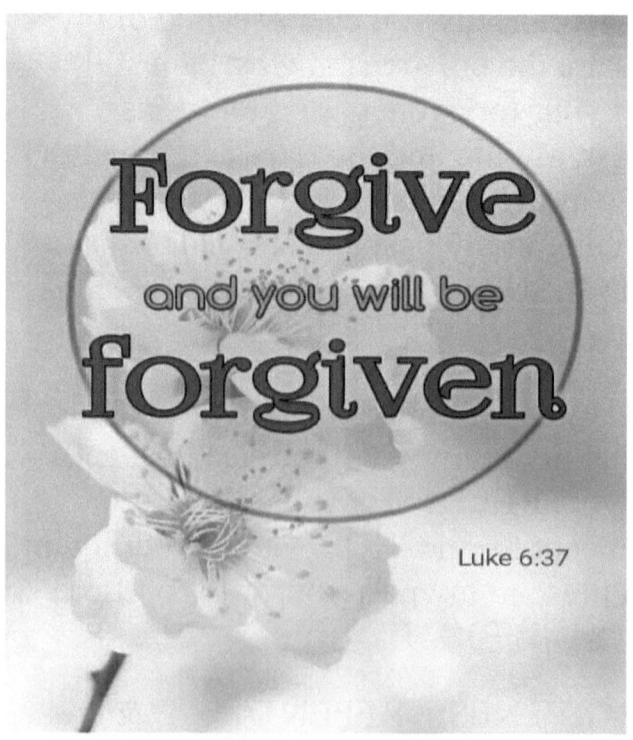
Forgive and you will be forgiven.
Luke 6:37

THE

BIBLE IS THERE TO LEAD YOU. GOD IS THERE
TO LOVE AND BRING YOU HOME.

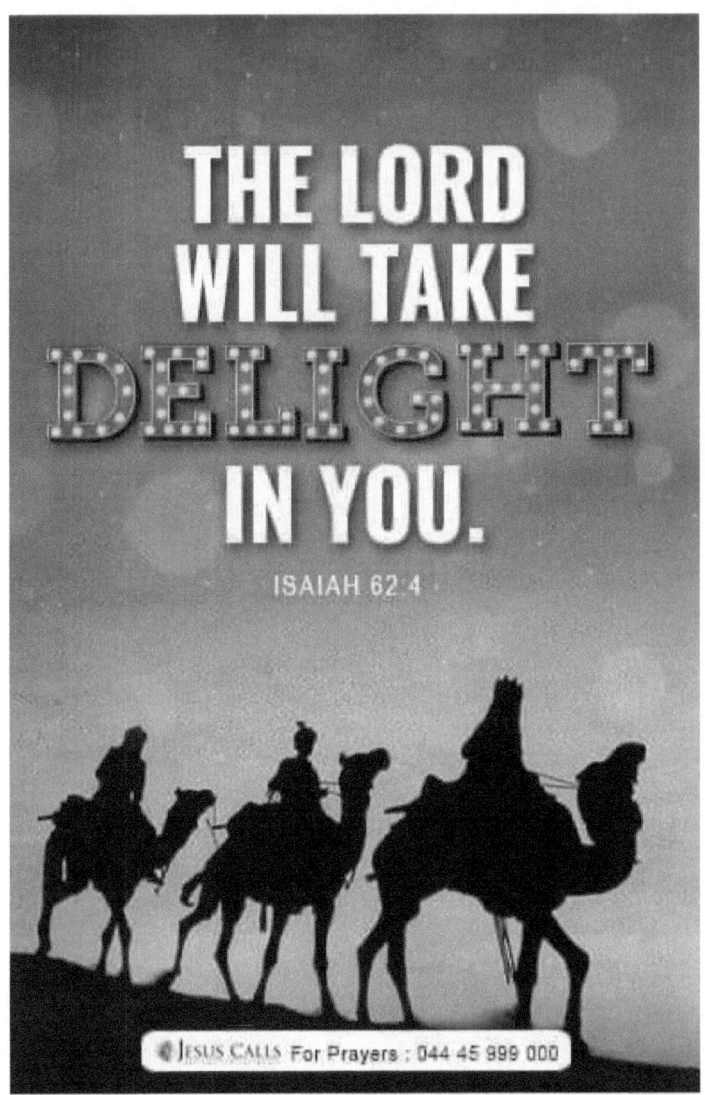

THE LORD
WILL TAKE
DELIGHT
IN YOU.
ISAIAH 62:4

Jesus Calls For Prayers : 044 45 999 000

BORN as one of us, lived among us, died for our
salvation and all God wants is for you to choose him,
love him and live for him. What will you choose?

Watch your life become easier. Help others
achieve peace and see your success with a new view.

There's always a way to change the
negative. Life isn't meant to be perfect or easy – but it
can be bearable if you try to always turn the negative

into a positive.

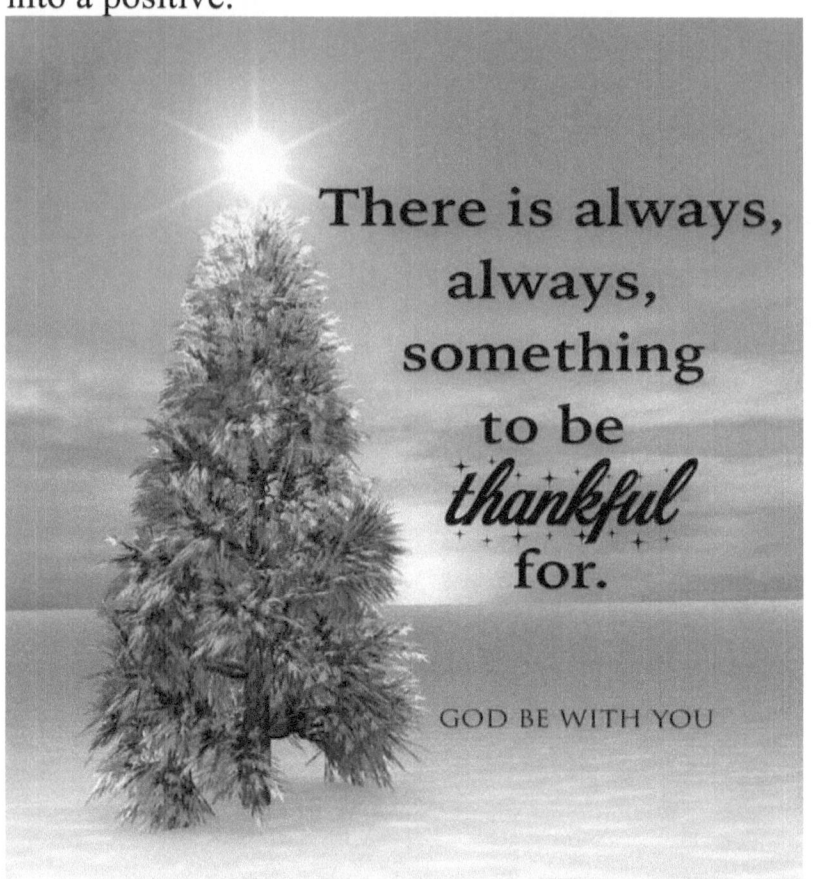

There is always, always, something to be *thankful* for.

GOD BE WITH YOU

Hardships exist, frustration is real but thankfulness helps you become aware that you never know what someone else is holding and what you can't see or they aren't showing could be far worse then what you have in life. Look beyond yourself to another sphere. I've learned that the most successful seem to have more scares then they realize. The mighty too shall fall – says the Lord. Envy, covetness, sloth and anger really holds people away from moving on. EVEN highy educated, worldly famed have weaknesses and flaws. Don't compare yourself with anyone because no one holds what you do.

Why envy something or wish for something that could be awful? Why focus on I've had a tough life and hold things within me. MOVE ON!

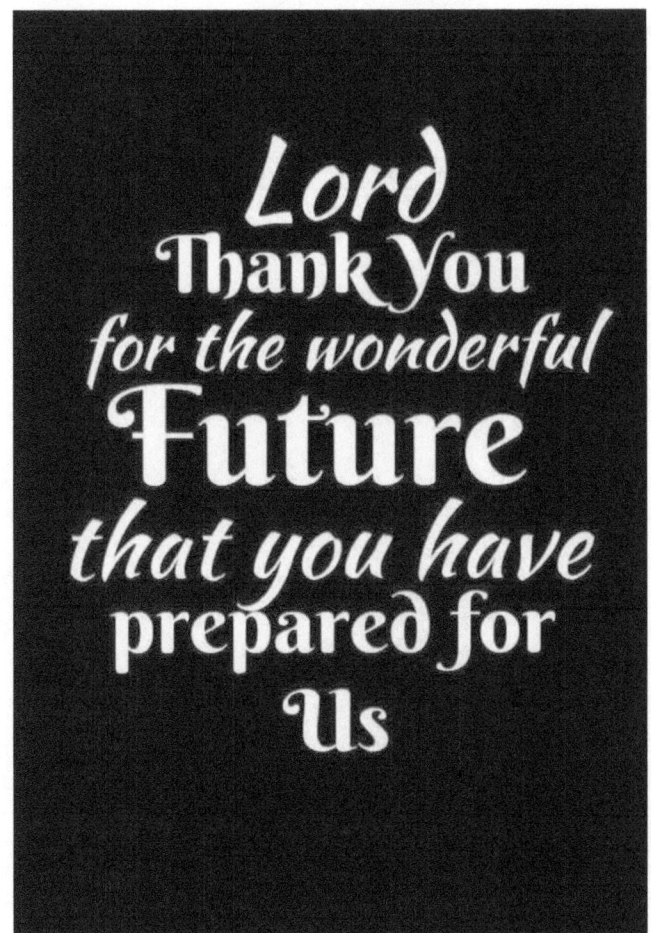

Lord
Thank You
for the wonderful
Future
that you have
prepared for
Us

MOVE ON TO YOUR GLORY. Write your story filled with GLORY AND PRAISE.

You will notice a peace within you when you are in the place where God wants you to be. Always take small steps and move forward. Never look back. God has it all.

Help bring the I CAN attitude back into AMERICA and get AMERICA back to the best version of what it should be. I CAN can be awesome will move the society to reach its full potential.

If I CAN change so can you. YOU CAN if you want to but that's your choice. AMERICA is waiting for your brave, brilliance to enhance and shine for extraordinary lives for everyone. You have the power within you to be magnificent – do it. Let your radiance shine and your life be under your control.

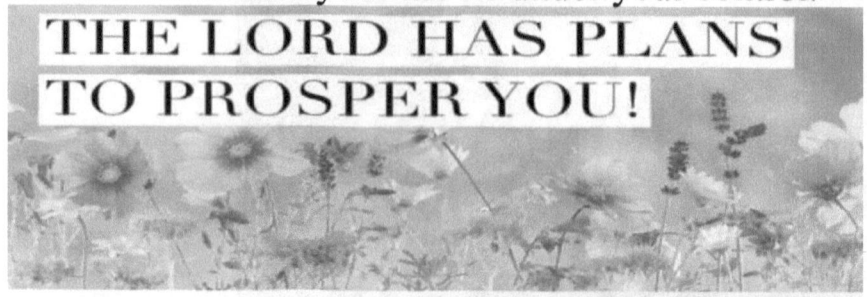

THE LORD HAS PLANS TO PROSPER YOU!

"For I know the plans I have for you," declares the Lord, "plans to prosper you and not to harm you, plans to give you hope and a future." -Jeremiah 29:11

You can do whatever you must in life, it's not easy for anyone. Throw away your past – it can't help you today. Your past is gone, done and over with all it can do is make you sad and prevent anything good. I pray this every day. Try it it may ease your pain.

Lord if I've ever been part of anyone's past that I need forgiveness I am seeking it here and repenting of it all here. I place myself fully into your care now. CONSUME ME LORD JESUS WITH ALL OF YOU AND ONLY WHAT'S MEANT TO BE FOR ME. CAST OUT ALL OF ME AND SHIELD ME FROM ALL THAT NOT MEANT FOR ME.

You must release all your negative to grow and achieve your greatness. It's hard, it hurts but saying goodbye and realizing your issues is the first step. Yes, we all fail and fall short. Especially me – but if you want to succeed you must use your past as a foundation for your future eternity.

Pray for all your issues and mistakes in life and those who caused them and move on.

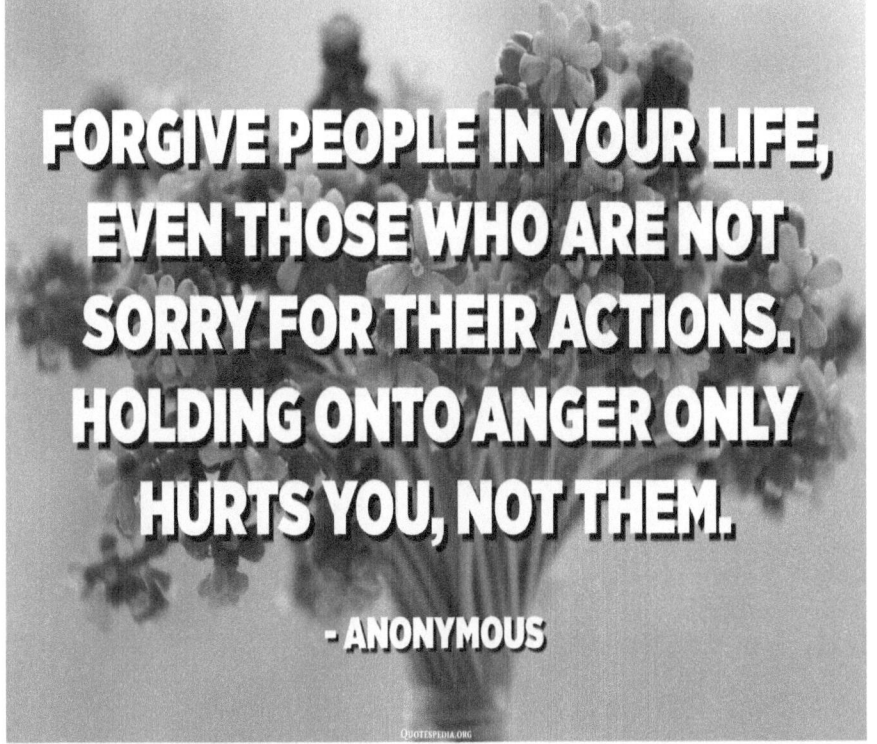

SET you soul free with forgiving no matter if you know where those who need to be forgiven are in the world, let God do the rest and see the peace come into your life fully. Jesus wants to restore you and make you whole. Jesus can set you free and show you a new side of you.

Believe me, I know how hard it is to let go. I struggle with it all the time and just through prayer realize fully that it's GOD that's in control and not me.

Forgiveness

Anyone can hold a grudge, but it takes a person with character to forgive. When you forgive, you release yourself from a painful burden. Forgiveness doesn't mean what happened was OK, and it doesn't mean that person should still be welcome in your life. It just means you have made peace with the pain, and are ready to let it go.

"What you believe will affect how you behave."

Dr. Bill Winston

www.billwinston.org

Some things in life will go and others you do learn to cope with on a different level when you let go.

It's fun to see the reaction on the doubters faces and fake friends. You learn quickly who not to ever be around and pray. I've chosen God's way not my way and my life is bearable. I am seeing a new me each day and am so grateful for God's help. I know

God will never let me down.

It's taken a long time for me and a lot of abuse and torment but; I'm helping others help themselves succeed as well. Miracles happen for all of us at different phases of life. HELP in life helps personally. Stay positive no matter what. Realize your issues and choices and why and accept ownership.

Help SAVE AMERICA, help save others if you can in life. THE GRATITUDE ATTITUDE is a first step to your success in life.

But because you are stubborn and refuse to turn away from your sin, you are storing up terrible punishment for yourself. For a day of wrath is coming, when God's righteous judgement will be revealed.

Romans 2:5

Let go before it's too late and feel the joy of being in the right realm of life.

Don't fight the past, don't fight your issues surrender them and march on to victory. Victory won by you with confidence, determination and steadfast commitment to yourself will be appreciated and valued more at the end of your life because you will be able to say, "I WAS IN CONTROL OF ALL OF IT WITH GOD'S HELP."

Be able to discern your Judas from your Peter. Peter had a bad day, Judas had a bad heart. Peter, you restore. Judas, you release. You got to know who to restore and who to release!

So many people in life need great roll models but find very few in their lives. My father was mine. Discover yours and think, hear, listen and practice the steps. Never be afraid to fall and stop worrying about opinions. Opinions don't matter in life only God's judgment.

Succeed on your own terms. If it's right for you then you must be happy and keep succeeding.

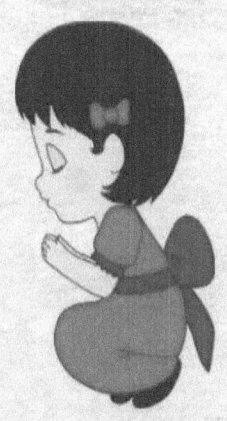

Sorry I'm not perfect but I'm not fake either.

via: fb.com/ShutUpImStillTalking

Nothing is Permanent.
Don't **stress** yourself
too much because
no matter how bad
the situation is...
It will change.

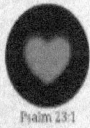

Psalm 23:1

NEVER EXPECT TO BE PERFECT BECAUSE YOU WILL NEVER ACHIEVE IT. IF it's ok with you that's what matters.

Experience what you must in life in a positive way. You are an awesome person with uniquely created gifts within you that no one in life possesses. May your light shine bright and your way forward be steadfast in glory for you.

Do your best with everything and never have regrets. If you hold regrets, fix them with confidence and positive motion.

Life is what you make it and all you need is God's acceptance. ASK FOR IT! RECEIVE IT and LET GO!

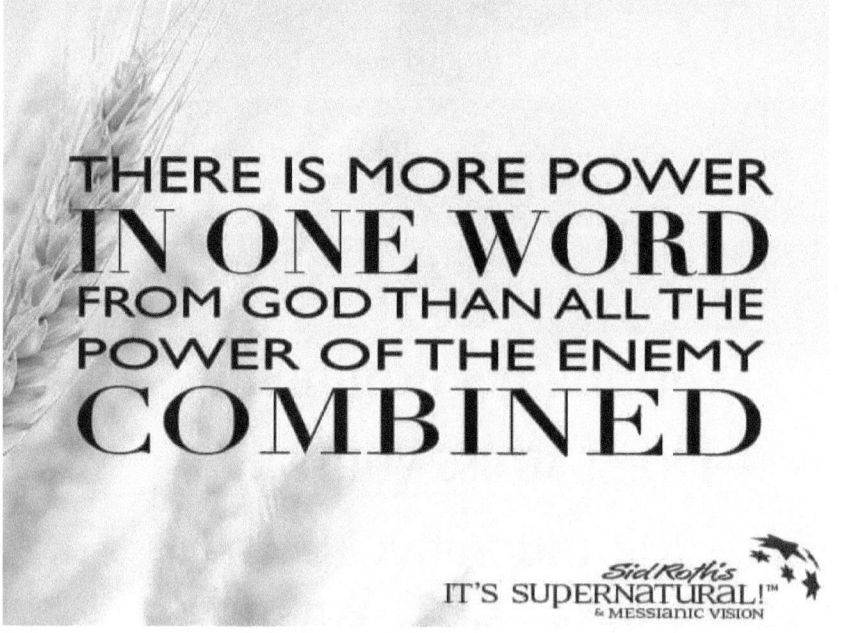

THERE IS MORE POWER IN ONE WORD FROM GOD THAN ALL THE POWER OF THE ENEMY COMBINED

Sid Roth's IT'S SUPERNATURAL!™ & MESSIANIC VISION

If you are moving in the right direction you will know it.

You will see it and you will feel it. The goodness is what's needed and with that stir in some greatness. What does this equal? YOU! Look in the mirror and see your beautiful soul.

Live life the best way possible and hold no one responsible but yourself and move on to what you feel is your personal greatness and success. Be proud of yourself, trust yourself and love yourself enough to keep on pursuing. Make your life a witness for all who see you. Make your moments a symbol of success and personal achievement. Make it all on your own and with no one restricting you.

Life is up to you. Saving your world can be mastered by each one of us meeting our own personal goals in life. BE A LIFE CHAIN FOR SOMEONE ELSE.

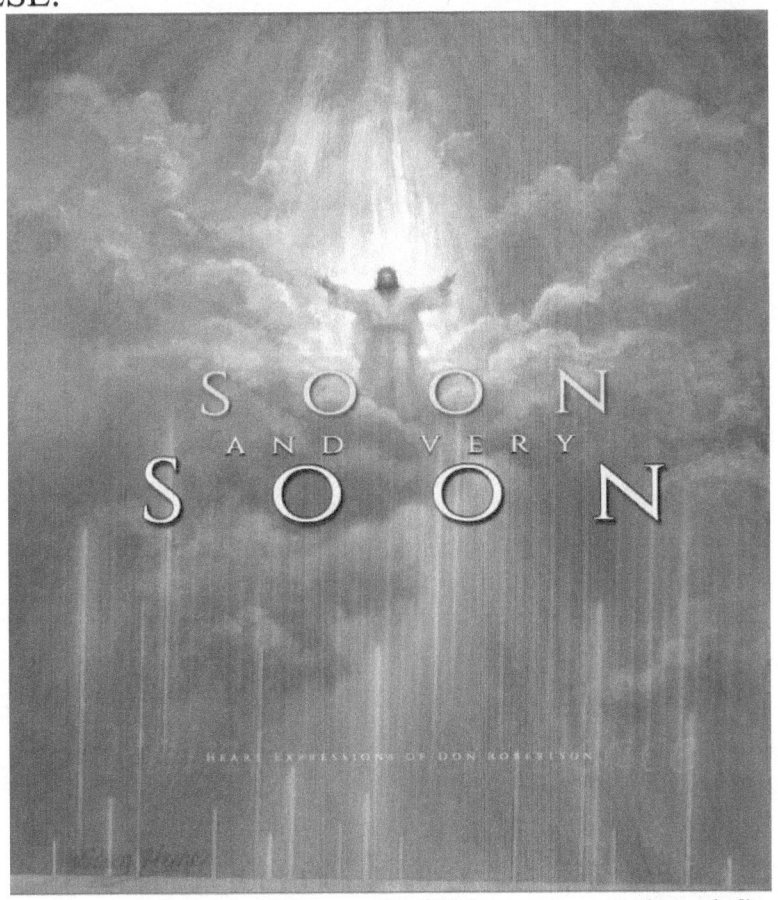

Live so that you will be accepted and find joy in the kingdom of God. Only you can master your journey. It's no one's fault but your own if you don't.

STOP DREAMING and start receiving. Work hard and never expect. This way you will never be disappointed in life. Too many people make too many open promises and NEVER produce.

Your mind will always
believe everything
you tell it.
Feed it faith.
Feed it truth.
Feed it with
Love.

Convince yourself to be awesome and achieve. Leave your mind free from what holds you back and move on.

Some people want material things. Me, I just want peace, happy times, and people who love me.

Realize your goals in the most positive way possible and remember no one's life is perfect, we all make mistakes but; we live through our journey. Others may appear to you as having had everything handed to them – but unless you are living inside them you do not know what they've had to bear in life. Yes, some people have more then others but; to those who much has been given much is expected of them.

Make sure you plant all your seeds on

good soil and fertilize them often with love. YOU REAP WHAT YOU SOW.

If you surround yourself with goodness – goodness will be achieved. If you make good choices – good things will be received. If you train yourself to never give up and succeed – eventually success will arrive. No one is perfect nor any better then anyone else no matter their wealth or list of accomplishments.

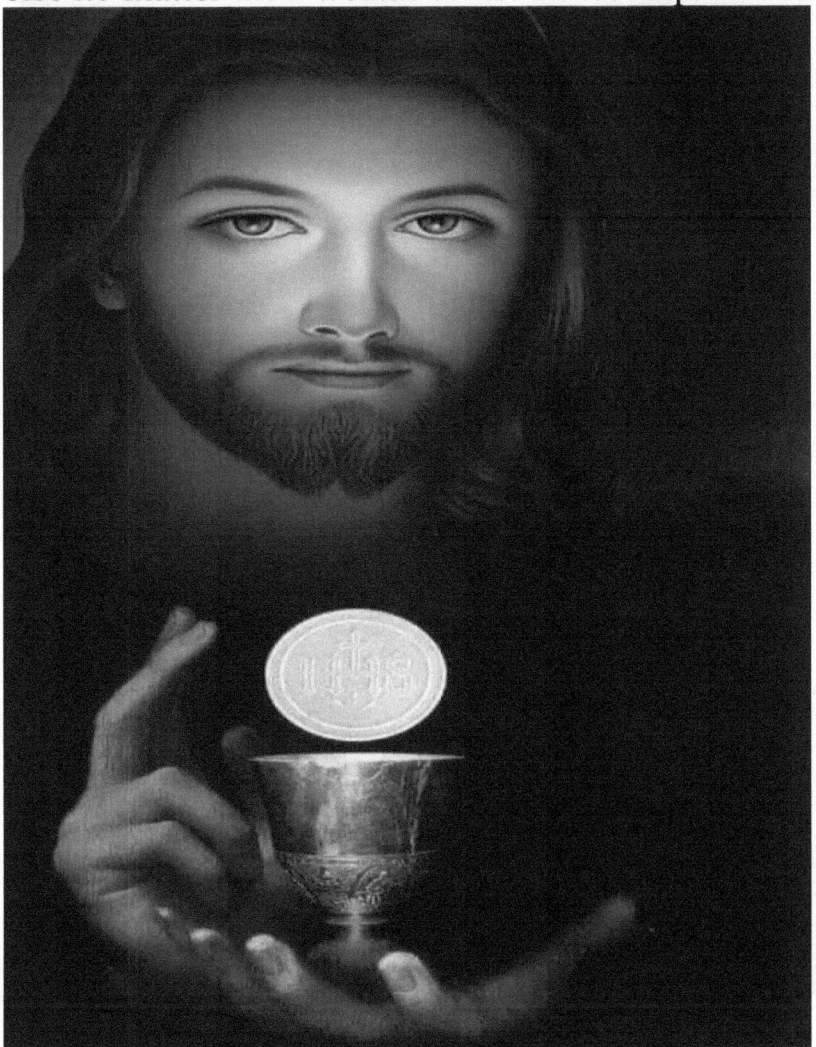

If you love yourself as you should you will make every effort possible to achieve the ultimate for yourself. No one can do it for you. If you eat my body and drink my blood I will abide in you and you in me.

A gift no one should refuse – but they do. WHAT ABOUT YOU?

> Let the Lord
> fight your battles.
> He hasn't lost
> one yet.

Life isn't a hand out and no, not everyone has it easy; not even if they look like the have had a plushy lifestyle. Be a fighter that wins not loses. Be a survivor who can march to their own beat and take the kudos as they come.

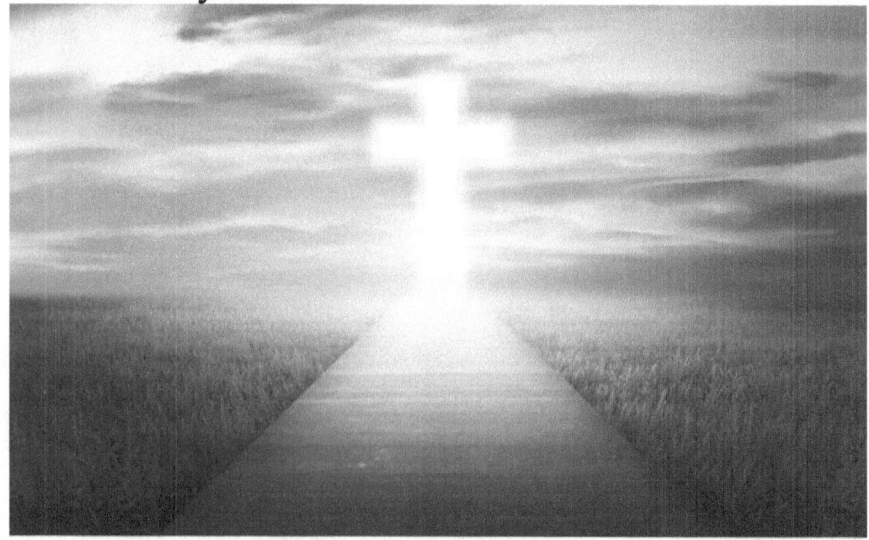

This journey is to prepare you for the other side of life. How are you going to live your journey? Make changes where they need to be made, live the way you should and be positive only. You know what your personal goals are and no one else does. Let go.

Life is too short for shoes that hurt your feet, friends that make you feel bad about yourself, and jobs that crush your soul.
Take a chance. Make a change.
The time is now.

Lisa Lewtan

Never look down on anyone because it could be you one day. It's all an option for you if you want it.

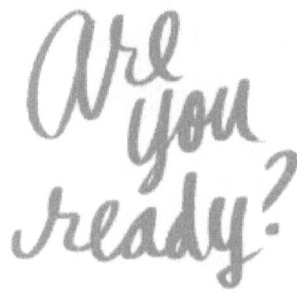

For all your goals you must achieve them and understand that if you remain positive and know what your goals are you can be victorious. BE VICTORIOUS WITH GOD TOO.

Your journey wasn't meant as a punishment it was meant to magnify you. Find your glory and write your story now. Let others learn and achieve from you.

You will enjoy the success if you achieve it. Why not listen to your own heart and those who honestly support you?

ARE YOU READY to reaceive your glory?

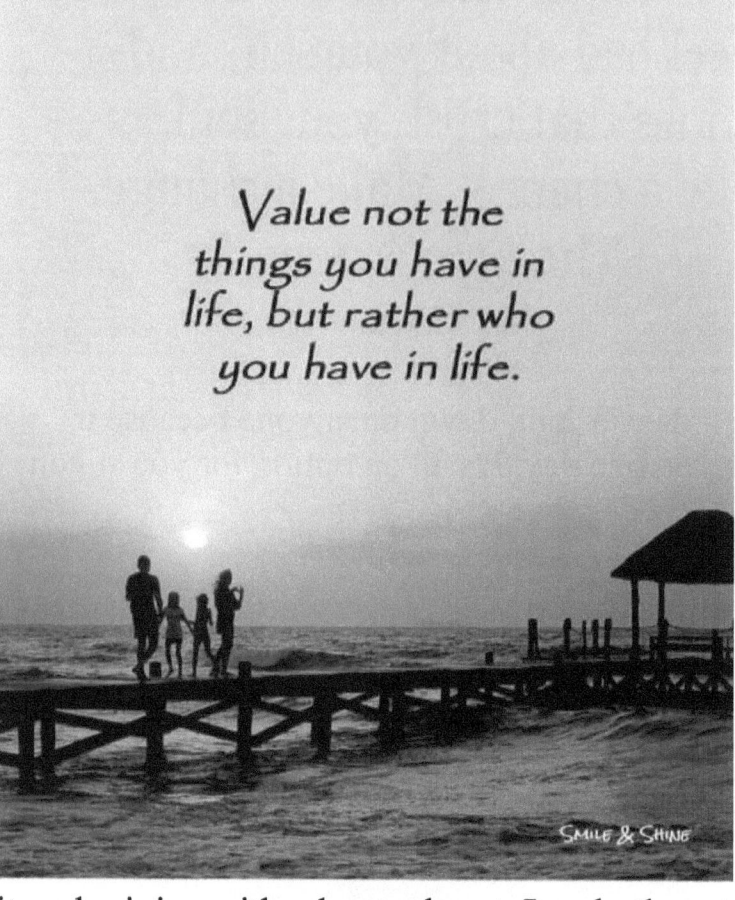

Value not the things you have in life, but rather who you have in life.

SMILE & SHINE

Claim it and rejoice with a happy heart. Lead others to their glory and never look back. The pain of yesterday and the past are gone and locked up. You can only use them as a foundation to never revert back.

With God all things are possible. I am learning TRUST now and LOVING MYSELF. You can too.

LIVE FOR A HIGHER BETTER PURPOSE THEN THE ONE YOU SEE IN FRONT OF YOU. For only God knows his plans for you and your greatness.

**Trust in God
for His plans
are bigger
than the ones
you have for
yourself.**

Let God teach you to TRUST like he's trying to teach me and believe in it as well. Your a great team when you are on GOD'S TEAM.

Part of trying to SAVE AMERICA and to SAVE YOU is to TRUST and let go. It's so hard when you've spent 90 per cent of your life not trusting, but with the help of good people surrounding you with great opportunities and kindness – you will succeed.

When you face your shadows, issues or querks head on – eliminate them one by one and reinforce it over and over again until you are sure they are gone. Stay positive no matter what.

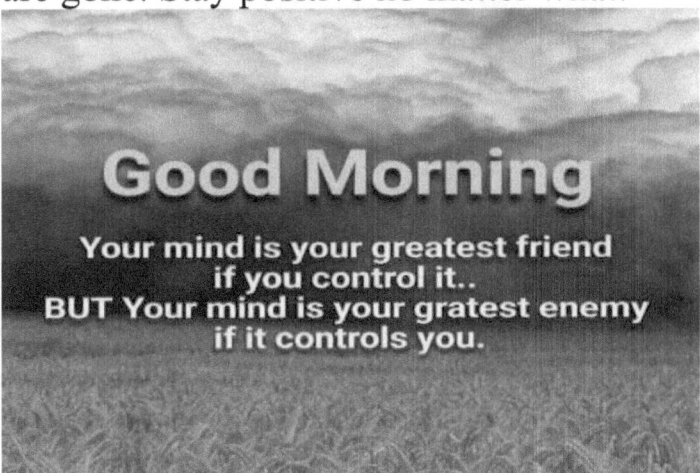

Good Morning

Your mind is your greatest friend
if you control it..
BUT Your mind is your gratest enemy
if it controls you.

BELIEVE in yourself and let God lead you onwards. You are made in the image and likeness of Jesus Christ - live a Christly life now.

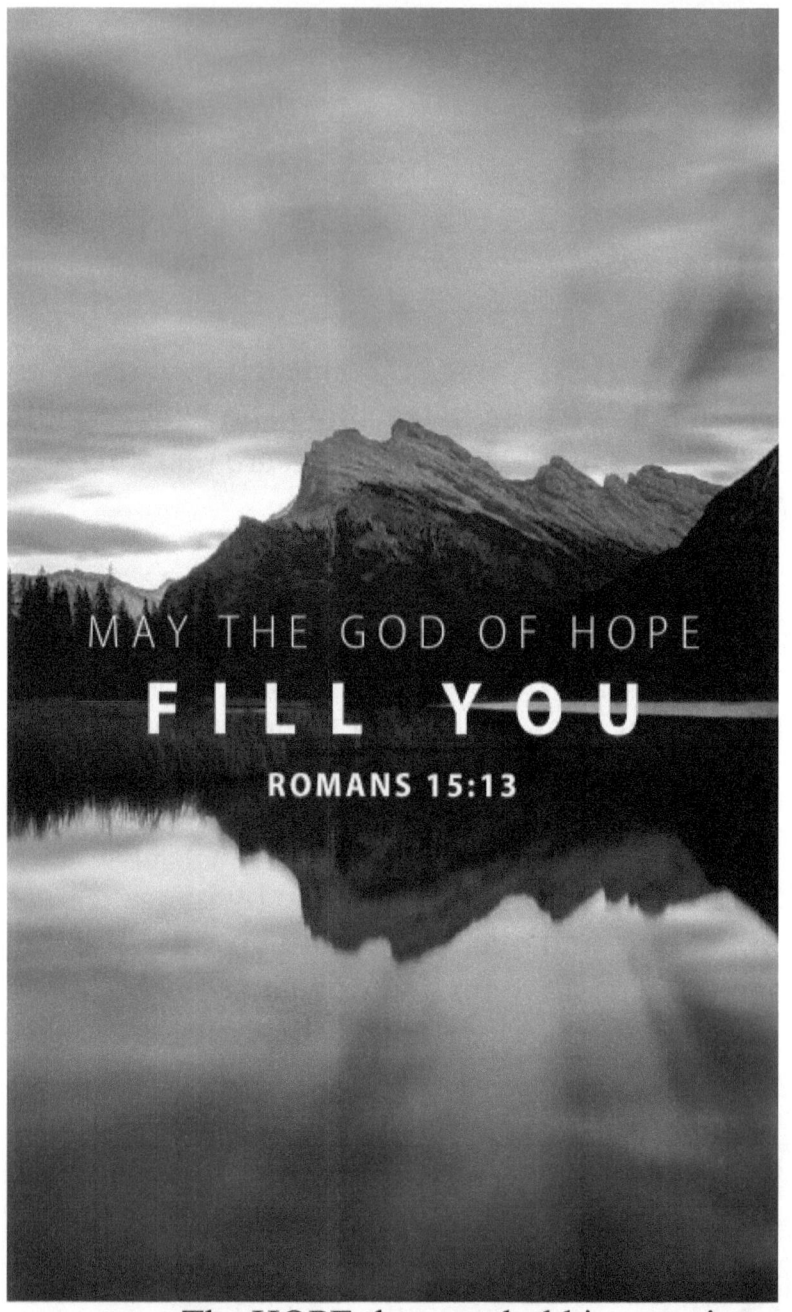

MAY THE GOD OF HOPE
FILL YOU
ROMANS 15:13

       The HOPE that you hold in your journey can only be achieved by positive moves forward resting in the Lord's hands. You must remove all your issues and live. God loves you and is wanting you to come home. BELIEVE in yourself and success. Let go. I am learning to let go and love myself too. Jesus is the love you need.

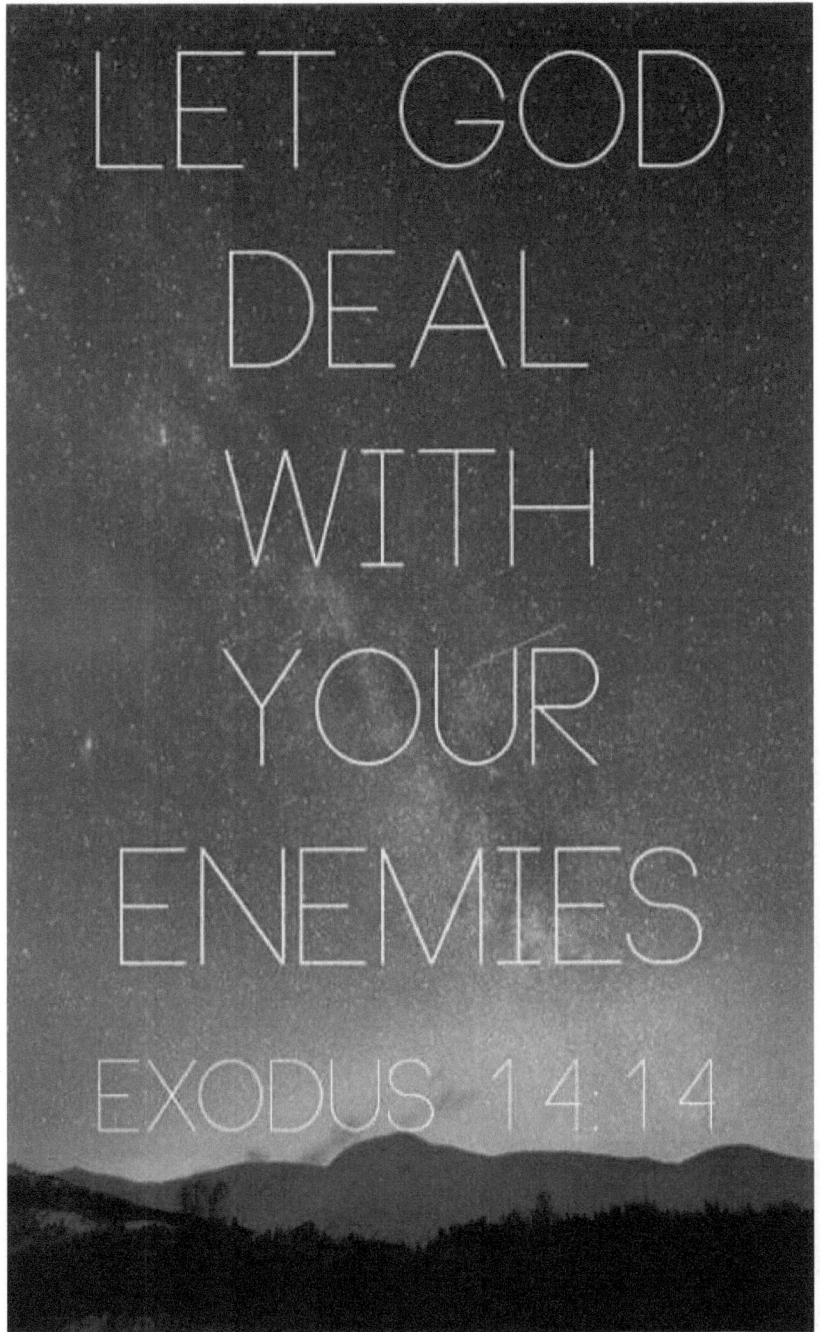

LET GOD DEAL WITH YOUR ENEMIES

EXODUS 14:14

The Lord has never lost a battle yet and he will never let you down. Trust him. I am learning to trust once again and it is awesome. You can see the favor of God in all your issues once you surrender fully to Jesus Christ. Your life will change for the absolute best but you must choose it.

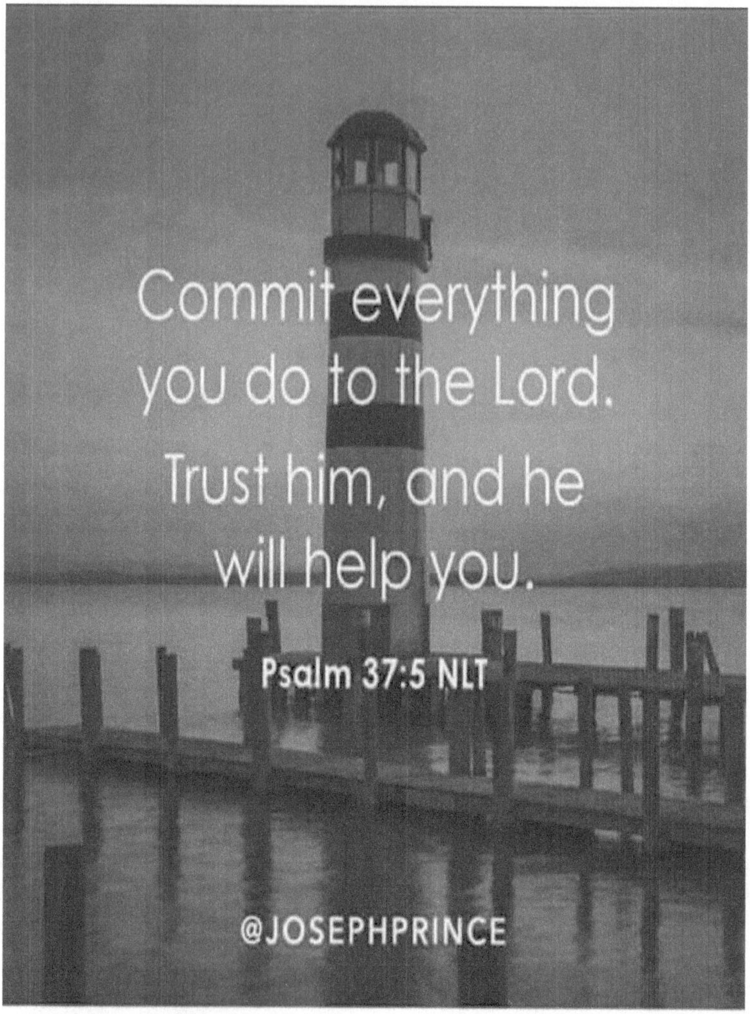

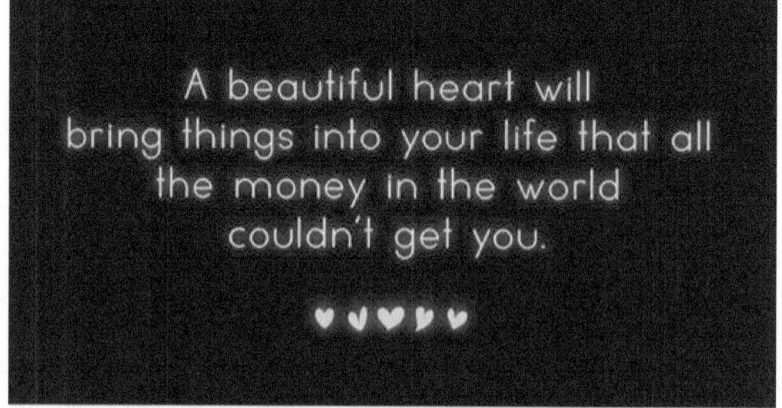

Commit everything
you do to the Lord.
Trust him, and he
will help you.

Psalm 37:5 NLT

@JOSEPHPRINCE

There's nothing any greater then God's love. See it in your life and never look back. Life will never be perfect but you will see the hand of God.

A beautiful heart will
bring things into your life that all
the money in the world
couldn't get you.

Remember the battle belongs to the Lord

and if you surrender yourself fully he will win it for you. Yes, your journey is a battle that Jesus can magnify try it now and release yourself fully.

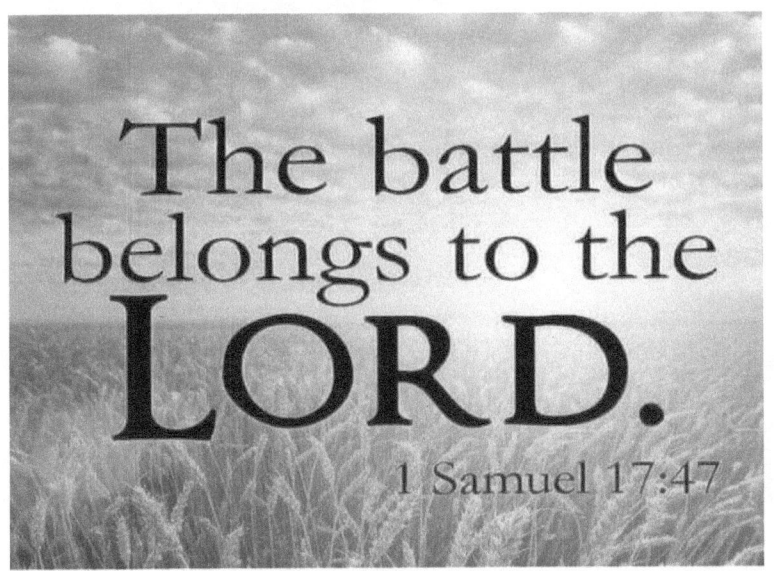

The battle belongs to the LORD.

1 Samuel 17:47

Call on him now. Receive him now and live for him. I am trying my hardest to myself. You can choose good or evil – I choose good JESUS and eternal life. COME FOLLOW ME SAYS THE LORD.

It's the best choice you will ever make in your life. Your free will allows you to choose him or to deny him. YOU must make the choice to accept JESUS CHRIST and fully commit to him.

Your eternal life depends on it. Believe in yourself strongly enough to choose and accept the consequences of that choice.

YOU CAN if I CAN so decide and stop procrastinating before its too late.

The love you are looking for is waiting for you in HEAVEN. The need to heal and be complete is within you. REACH FOR THE LORD and receive.

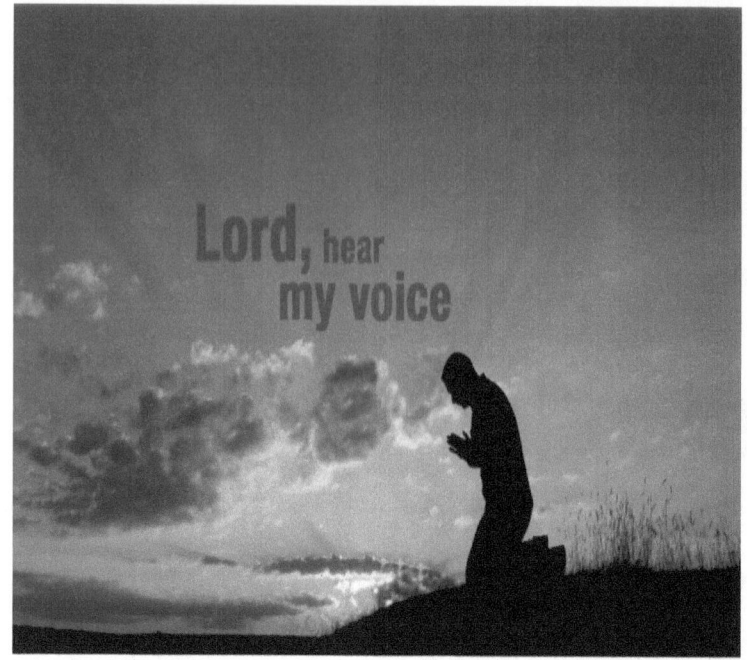

Lord grant me the needs I have to come to you and keep me ever mindful of your presence. Lead me to be an example not an excuse and use me to fulfill your needs in this world.

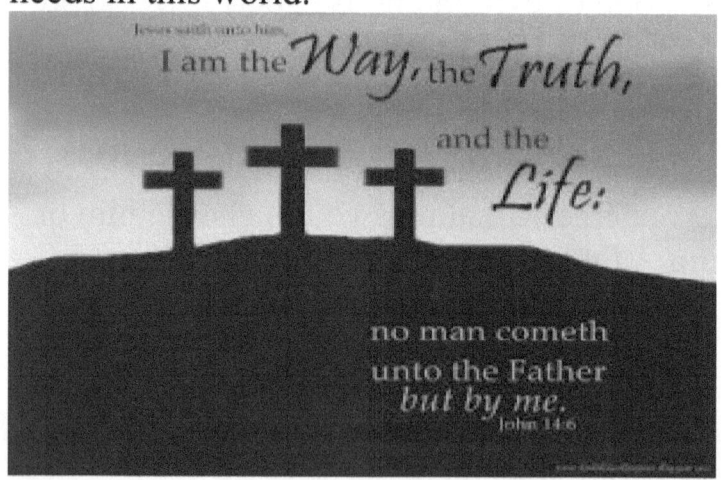

Fold your hands and kneel in prayer and accept the love so that you can be a witness to others. Jesus Christ needs real warriors who will fight for him with no hesitation and be TRUE to his word – THE BIBLE.

Everyone has different issues and needs and different approaches to their needs. Be patient, be quiet, be alluring and compassionate in all your witness. RUB THE LOVE IN and SCRUB THE LOVE OUT.

We are all children of God's and are called to love one another as I have loved you – says the Lord. Figure out the best approach and achieve it. No one will be looked down upon by our HEAVENLY FATHER.

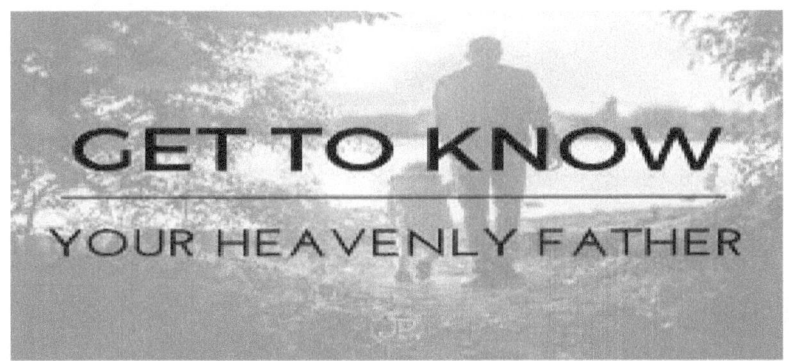 He is waiting for you to come to him and be all that you can be. You were made in the image and likeness of his only begotten son and you are a brother or sister of JESUS CHRIST. What more could you ever ask for in life?

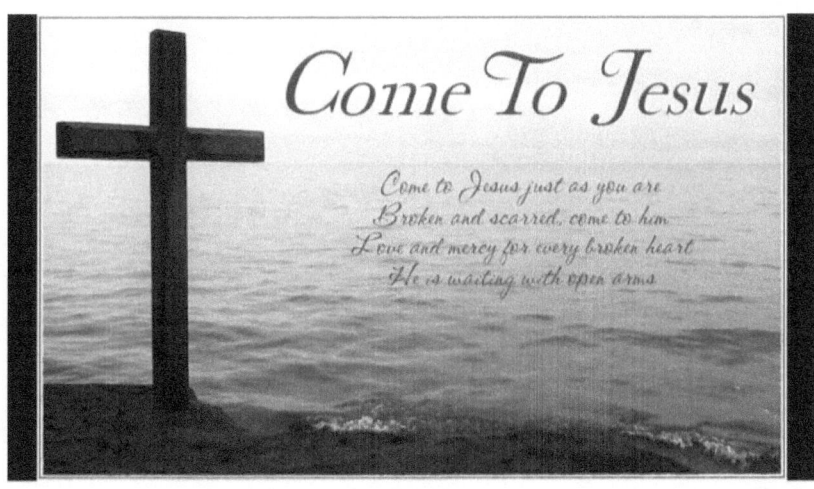

THANK YOU JESUS FOR LOVING ME.

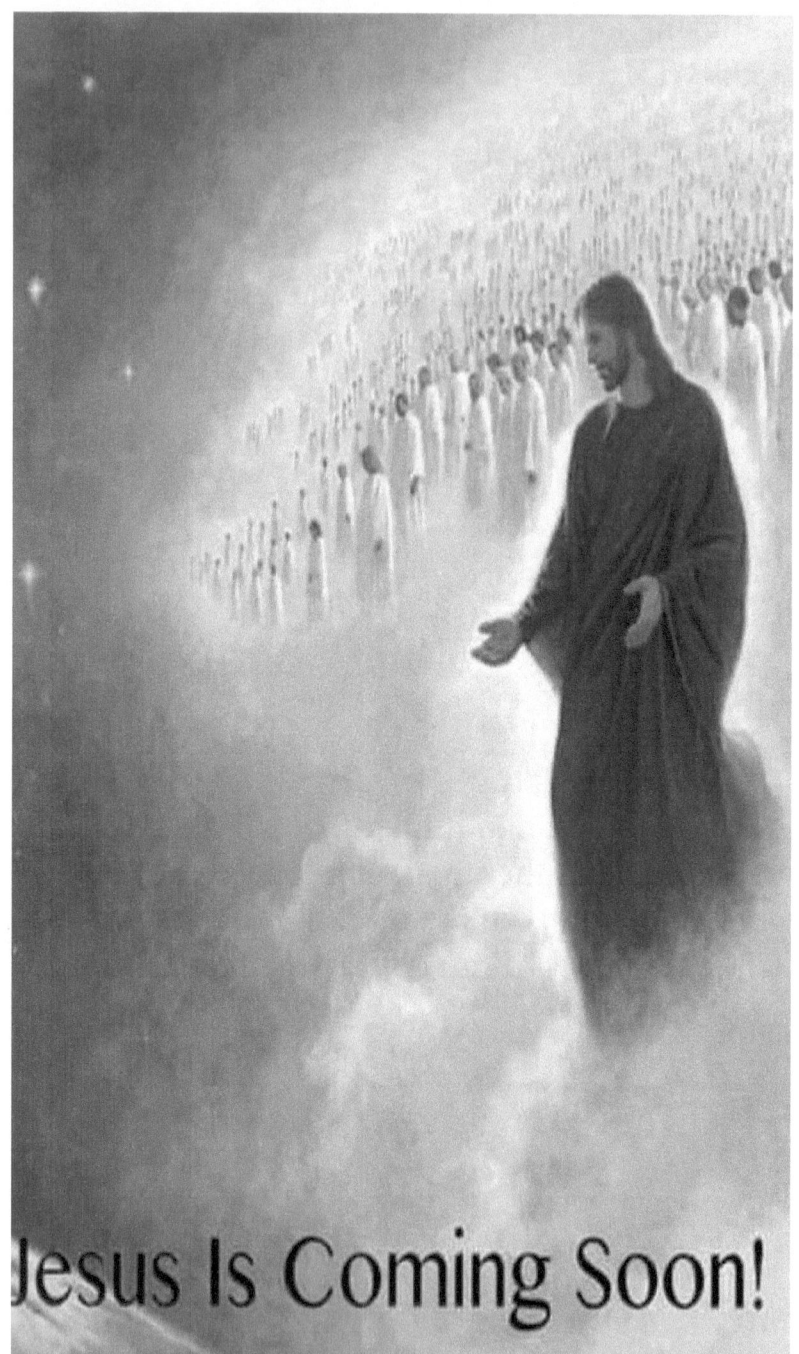

Jesus Is Coming Soon!

Author: Linda Lee